NOT ALL WHO WANDER (SPIRITUALLY) ARE LOST

NOT ALL WHO WANDER (SPIRITUALLY) ARE LOST

(A STORY OF CHURCH)

TRACI RHOADES

FOREWORD BY JERUSALEM GREER

Church Publishing
19 East 34th Street
New York, NY 10016
www.churchpublishing.org

Cover design by Paul Soupiset
Typeset by PerfecType, Nashville, Tennessee

Library of Congress Cataloging-in-Publication Data

Names: Rhoades, Traci, author.
Title: Not all who wander (spiritually) are lost : a story of church / Traci Rhoades ; foreword by Jerusalem Greer.
Identifiers: LCCN 2019045501 (print) | LCCN 2019045502 (ebook) | ISBN 9781640652798 (paperback) | ISBN 9781640652804 (epub)
Subjects: LCSH: Spirituality--Christianity. | Church.
Classification: LCC BV4501.3 .R459 2020 (print) | LCC BV4501.3 (ebook) | DDC 248.4--dc23
LC record available at https://lccn.loc.gov/2019045501
LC ebook record available at https://lccn.loc.gov/2019045502

To all the people who have gone to church with my mom,
my daughter, and me

Contents

Foreword

At the time that this book is being published, the United States, and the American experience of Christianity, is in a bit of an upheaval. Or a complete disintegration. Or a renewal. We aren't sure just yet, as the battles—cultural, political, religious—are still being waged. There are so many divisions and schisms that it is hard to keep track of who is for what or what is for who. All too often, discussions of Christian faith are held in terse exchanges over social media, with the goal being not to learn, not to listen, but to win.

Into this fray came Traci, with her simply stated questions on Facebook and Twitter, asked in her agenda-free tone. Questions such as "For those of you who know, what does your church do with the leftover Communion elements?" or "Do you own a prayer book?" and "Did you attend a youth group? And if so, give me a memory." And, without drama or rancor, people shared their responses, they told their stories, they passed along memories and anecdotes, and they even asked their own questions. Civil—even charming—discourse was the norm. By offering her own holy curiosity as a gift, Traci created a safe space for people, in all stages and expressions of Christian faith, to speak and to be heard.

This book is a lovely extension of that space. A gathering of stories and experiences from a wide variety of voices, all beautifully woven together, with Traci's own story of spiritual wandering and discovery as the binding thread. Her story is a story that can teach all of us a little bit more about what it means—and why it matters—to be curious about and open to how the Holy Spirit speaks and moves in the lives of all people. This book is for anyone on a faith exploration themselves, looking for encouragement and hope instead of battles and absolutes.

As someone whose own faith journey has been marked both by adventurous wandering and wondering, and who, when lost in the wilderness, looked for signs that not all was lost, I am so glad to share this book with you. May we all find our way home at last.

Jerusalem Jackson Greer
Preservation Acres
2020

Introduction: Let's Be Friends

"Not all those who wander are lost."

—J. R. R. Tolkien, *The Fellowship of the Ring*

I pull into the church parking lot about ten minutes early, and it occurs to me if I go in now I might have to mingle with strangers. I decide to wait.

Out of the corner of my eye, I see another car pull up a few spaces down. A man hurriedly gets out, robe in hand, throwing a white collar around his neck. Approximately six minutes before the Ash Wednesday service will start, the priest arrives. I open my car door, and he gestures in my general direction, smiling ever so slightly.

The first thing a visitor notices in a Catholic church is its beauty. This particular church is only a few years old, so its stained-glass windows still sparkle like new, showing no sign of fading from the sun. The exposed wooden beams on the ceiling speak to the rustic northern town where the parish is in ministry.

Stepping into the nave, I dip my finger in the holy water because I can never resist it. Every time I reach for that water, I envision a siren going off at my touch: "Protestant alert!" Nevertheless, I keep going; the water holds such symbolic significance in the Bible, and I love feeling the moistness on my fingers, signaling to my heart that it's time for worship. Quickly, I cross myself. Still no siren. Every time it's worth the risk.

I take an aisle seat on the last row. There are about thirty faithful ones at the service: The beautiful older lady wearing a black mantilla; the gentleman who genuflects before accepting the communion elements. Not many children. Then I see Jeanne, a dear friend I know from the Reformed church I attend in the next town over. What a wonderful feeling to find a familiar face in the crowd.

Suddenly, I hear a voice behind me: "Will you hold this for me just a second, please?"

I turn to see the man I encountered in the parking lot. The priest. He needs to put on his wireless mic, so he hands me the small bowl filled with ashes. I am holding last year's Palm Sunday branches, now burned up and ground into sacred bits. The ashes rest in my hands. I think to myself, "What if I dropped these right now?"

The service offers several moments of complete silence. Not an uncomfortable silence, but a prayer shawl of sorts you could slide over your head, blocking out the noise of our world and aiding the holiness of the moment. This sacred silence brings me to tears that morning. It feels like something I have been missing all my life without even knowing it.

It comes time to receive the ashes. The Catholics invite me to join them in this act of penance. We're all sinners who need to repent and recognize our great need for a Savior. Everyone—Catholics, Orthodox, and Protestants alike—agrees on that.

"Remember that you are dust, and to dust you shall return."

More tears. The feeling of the priest's fingers as he swiped the ash cross on my forehead. I'd never received a blessing like this before. Although it reminded me of my need for penance, it felt every bit like a blessing. He made the sign of the cross on me; symbolizing the marking I already have because I belong to Jesus.

I sat silently in prayer as others (everyone else?) went forward for communion. This concluded the church service.

As I left, the priest stood at the door to greet those in attendance. I told him this was my first Ash Wednesday service. He said, "Are you Catholic?" I said, "No." He smiled, and then assured me, "It's OK. We can still be friends."

Growing up, Mom took us to church but Dad didn't go. The most important man in my life up to that point, but he didn't share my faith journey with me. Dad didn't get religion. Perhaps there was too much baggage in his life to "let go and let God," as they say. I saw firsthand a life lived with God and church (my mom's) and a life lived without God or church (my dad's). I have never doubted which one seemed right and true to me.

I love the church and I'll never walk away, but we could do better. The next time you're reading in the Gospels, take note of how Jesus communicates. He asks a lot of questions and he tells a lot of stories. This book does that. I think doing these things will help us be a more loving church. The longer I walk this Christian path, and I've got more than a few years on me now, I think what the priest expressed to me at my first Ash Wednesday service is true. Church, I believe it deep within me, even in these tumultuous times, we can still be friends.

Apostles' Creed (ca. 700 AD)

I believe in God, the Father almighty,
maker of heaven and earth;
And in Jesus Christ his only Son our Lord;
who was conceived by the Holy Ghost,
born of the Virgin Mary,
suffered under Pontius Pilate,
was crucified, dead, and buried.
He descended into hell.
The third day he rose again from the dead.
He ascended into heaven,
and sitteth on the right hand of God the Father almighty.
From thence he shall come to judge the quick and the dead.
I believe in the Holy Ghost,
the holy catholic Church,
the communion of saints,
the forgiveness of sins,
the resurrection of the body,
and the life everlasting. Amen.

Chapter 1

Safe and Secure

Two churches raised me. I like to think God was telling me from the beginning that it wouldn't be just one Christian tradition for me. We moved to my childhood home in rural Missouri when I was three years old. The first Southern Baptist President, Jimmy Carter, was moving into the White House at the same time we were settling in to our three-bedroom ranch-style house, also white in color.

I say I grew up Southern Baptist, but I realize now there was a strong Methodist influence as well. Mt. Olive United Methodist Church was just up the road from my house. I knew this church intimately. Many a sticky summer day, my brothers and I would ride our bikes or walk the dogs to the church and back. There was also a cemetery across the road from that church and we would wander up and down the rows of tombstones. I'm not sure we ever forget the churches of our childhood and how they shaped us.

I always felt comfortable in Mt. Olive's sanctuary. The Holy Spirit dwelled there. Sometimes the Spirit appears as a cloud by day and fire by night. Water can symbolize the Spirit's presence. A mighty wind. A whisper. Personally, the Holy Spirit met me at Mt. Olive Church repeatedly during my childhood. Though never taking the form of an actual image, I felt that strong, comforting presence.

The church never locked its doors. I'd run up the outdoor stairs to the red front doors, opening them into a small foyer. I always wondered who thought to put the wooden swinging doors between the foyer and the sanctuary. A smart individual who realized swinging doors wouldn't make as much noise when a squirmy child has to be taken out of the service—an experience I knew all too well.

I spent hours playing church at Mt. Olive. Can anyone say that about a church anymore? I'd play the piano with a hymn book on the music rack and give mock sermons to any stuffed animals or dolls I'd brought along. Of course, there was always an altar call at the end. Altars have always held deep meaning for me as the place where I do my most important work with God.

Although this church was geographically closest, it wasn't the church where we placed our membership. Our neighbor, Mary Emma, invited us to attend a small Southern Baptist church with her. At Mt. Pleasant, we had Juanita at the piano. She played mostly by ear and kept her own unique rhythm. The hymn might go from fast to slow to fast again. One had to be ready. Some of my childhood favorites included "Victory in Jesus," "Sweet Hour of Prayer," and "When We Walk with The Lord." We don't sing those hymns much anymore.

Like any church, we had our own version of what I call "church aerobics." We'd start out standing, as Juanita played a few songs. The preacher would pray. We'd sit down for a while after that. Listen to announcements. To switch up the mood, we'd sing a slower song. Often, there would be special music as we passed the offering plate. Another prayer, followed by the sermon. At the end of the sermon, we'd stand to sing one more song, called the "invitation hymn." The pastor would ask questions. Perhaps he'd ask if anyone, by a show of hands, realized they needed to forgive someone else. No peeking. Or did they have a worry they were holding on to that the Lord was asking them to surrender? But the primary question was always this: have you asked Jesus to be your Lord and Savior?

Every Sunday, we were expected to wrap up and be out the door in one hour.

My family started attending Mt. Pleasant about the time the church got a new pastor. He had grown up in the area, so many already knew him. I couldn't have realized it at the time but the influence Chuck and his family would have on me would extend far beyond the walls of this country church.

His son Jesse was my first church friend and wherever he happened to be on a Sunday morning, fun was sure to follow. Toward the end of the service, Chuck would ask people with wedding anniversaries or birthdays to come forward so we could sing to them as they put a mission offering in a set of designated tin cans.

Jesse, about four years old at the time, said he had an anniversary every week. When you're a toddler, some jokes never get old. He'd raise his hand and start to run up the aisle. His mom would reach for his belt buckle and yank him back. Hilarious.

Flannel boards, vacation Bible school, being an angel in the Christmas plays, children's choir, kids' sermons—I remember it all. Our church averaged about fifty people a week. The earliest verse I remember learning speaks to the relationship I've always had with the church. I can't find this exact paraphrase in any of my Bibles but I do believe it's how Evelyn, my childhood Sunday school teacher, taught it: "I was glad when they said unto me, 'Let us go to church.'" (Psalm 122:1)

I am saddened when I hear of those who experienced so much difficulty in their childhood days at church. Legalism. Abuse. Lies. Judgment. Cult movements. It shouldn't be that way. I want to start out addressing this important reality. If your experience with church is drastically dissimilar from mine, I see you. I'm sorry for the ways this human institution has hurt you. Christ doesn't hurt. His conviction is instructive, not destructive, in nature. He promises if we come to him, we can share in his easy yoke and lightened burdens. It doesn't mean our lives suddenly become perfect, but he walks beside us through it all. In sharing my story and what I, along with others, have realized from our varied experiences as believers, I hope we'll better understand the good that happens when we come to him together.

The people of Mt. Pleasant raised me up in the faith, just as my play times within the wooden structure at Mt. Olive surely contributed. I hope you'll come to realize, in spite of any cynicism or bitterness you might harbor toward church, you've been touched somewhere along the way by Christians who are good and faithful servants. They are easy for me to identify because when I sit among these men and women, my breathing steadies, my soul relaxes. Regardless of their circumstances, they have a joy and a peace about them. I knew from a very young age I wanted to exhibit these qualities in my own life. I counted on these people to show me how to do that.

Some of the best memories I have from those early days at church include our times in the church basement eating together. Baptists are known for their potlucks, and they do come by this fame honestly. The first half of the buffet line was filled with crockpots and casserole dishes (macaroni and cheese, a pasta dish of some sort or—my favorite—meatloaf). Moving down the line, you'd hit Tupperware Lane, with salads of the green, pasta, and Jello variety. Next, bread or rolls, green bean casseroles, and cheesy potatoes. By then, your plate was filled to overflowing so you'd come back for dessert. No one ever skipped dessert, of course. In Isaiah 25:6, we read about a day when our Lord will prepare a feast. It mentions choice meat and finely aged wine. In my mind at least, there will also be endless supplies of cold fried chicken and orange Jello fluff.

These days when I ponder the theological connections between food and church, I turn to one of my favorite writers. In her book, *Bread and Wine*, Shauna Niequist writes, "When you eat, I want you to think of God, of the holiness of hands that feed us, of the provision we are given every time we eat. When you eat bread and you drink wine, I want you to think about the body and the blood every time, not just when the bread and wine show up in church, but when they show up anywhere—on a picnic table or a hardwood floor or a beach."

I was fortunate to have a number of Christians in my extended family as well (also good cooks). In my junior high years, Mom's dad, Granddad Bennett, started behaving strangely, once our family had gathered for Christmas. In those days, the aunts brought a few side dishes while Grandma did the rest of the cooking. At one point, Granddad conspiratorially leaned in toward a group of us and said, "I don't know who that woman is in the kitchen but she's been working real hard all day."

Eventually we received a diagnosis. Granddad had Alzheimer's disease, an illness we didn't know much about at the time. Eventually he went from his farm to a rest home in town. One visit to see him stands out in my mind. As we were saying our goodbyes, a nurse approached us. "Watch this," she said. Pushing the bench away, she rolled Granddad's wheelchair over to a piano, placing his hands on the keys. He played mostly by ear and started hitting the notes with incredible familiarity. Then he started singing along. He couldn't have told us his name or who any of us were, but he knew every word to the old hymns he sang that day. "In the Sweet By and By," "I'll Fly Away." Even when our minds are hopelessly forgetful, the heart remembers.

I realized this for myself when I became a mother. I'd often rock my daughter to sleep in a rocking chair, with the back and forth rhythm lulling me to sleep as well. My voice would go on autopilot, and I'd find myself singing hymns from my childhood, "Only trust him, only trust him, only trust him now; he will save you, he will save you, he will save you now." I didn't know all the words to the verses as Granddad did, but the songs were there inside of me. The heart remembers.

A few months after that visit, we got the call Granddad had passed away, and my mom met up with her mom, sisters, and brother at the funeral home to make the necessary arrangements. I headed to Mt. Olive. Since the church never closed, I knew I could kneel at its altar for as long as I needed to. No one would mind. That day, I poured my heart out to Jesus. I missed a man I called Granddad. I knew how sad this was going to make my mom, so I prayed for her too. Sometimes it was the people of God who loved me well. Other times, it was the church building itself.

The people of God, our church family, also stepped in to help during our time of grieving. If you've ever been loved on by a church when a family member has passed away, you know how much their kindnesses mean. I saw my church family in the crowd of people at Granddad's funeral, and I knew we had their support. A few years later, when Mom would lose her younger brother in a tragic car accident, these same people would walk alongside us again. We couldn't make sense of all this sorrow but as my aunt sang at Granddad's funeral, "Farther along we'll know all about it; farther along we'll understand why. So, cheer up my brother, live in the sunshine; we'll understand it all by and by."

Although Mom grew up in church, she didn't have a personal salvation experience until she was already a mother and in her early twenties. She was a baby Christian alongside her children and had a *Living Bible* in those days. Even before I could read, I thumbed through her Bible because it made me feel grown up. One day, I must have decided since I was looking through it, the Bible was partly mine too, because I wrote my name in it in big, childish letters. That made her mad.

A few years ago, a new woman joined my Bible study. Guess what Bible she brought with her? That same olive green, hardcover *Living Bible.* I've since learned it was popular in the seventies, released amidst great controversy as a modern paraphrased Bible, much like the controversy that surrounded Eugene Peterson's *The Message,* which was published in my adult years. While I don't recommend using Bibles like this as your primary reading Bible, I have found these versions to be a helpful resource in gaining fresh insight into passages that are difficult to understand. I know the *Living Bible* helped my mother along tremendously in her early days as a Christian.

The churches, the Bibles, the people, all precious parts of my childhood. I received a private message from a childhood friend on social media a few years ago now. "Traci Dawn" (back home, many people called me that to keep from confusing me with my dad, also named Tracy), he wrote, "we were at Mt. Pleasant this afternoon. They were nice enough to host a lunch for our family. My grandfather's funeral was today and he's buried at Mt. Olive."

It took me back instantly: The red, scratchy carpet on the stairs. They would have served the meal in the wide-open meeting space in the basement. I wondered if the classrooms were still partitioned off by makeshift walls. I admit, I was more than a little jealous he had gone back. I hadn't been there since 1991.

He continued, "It felt strange being in the basement and taking the stairs up to the sanctuary. Lots of memories of summers with you many years ago!" It must have felt strange indeed to him, for these days he lives in large cities like New York and Dallas. He concluded, "That's what made us who we are today." Yes, when a tiny little church on a gravel road in the middle of nowhere takes you in its arms and you feel every ounce of love offered up in that embrace, you don't ever forget it.

It was a sunny summer day when I gave my life to Jesus. I did it the same way Southern Baptists have done it for hundreds of years. I'd already had a number of conversations with my mom about what it meant to "be saved." I white-knuckled the pew in front of me for the first few verses of "Just as I Am." Good thing there are six verses. I closed my eyes and silently asked God to help me make my way to the front even though my knees were wobbly. I released my death grip on the pew and pointed my right foot forward, meeting Pastor Mike up front. There, at seven years old, I prayed the sinner's prayer with my pastor.

If you're paying close attention, you might be asking yourself what happened to Pastor Chuck. Well, as a congregation, we were asking ourselves that very question. I was young so I didn't understand the details, but Chuck had resigned as pastor of our church. He'd taken a position as youth pastor at the First Baptist Church in town. Pastor Mike took his place. Even though I would have preferred Chuck baptize me, Mom and I agreed it would be best to keep the peace and go with Mike.

Our church was small and didn't have a baptistry so a few weeks later I was baptized at the First Baptist Church. Dad wasn't there, but I don't remember noticing because I was surrounded by the faithful of my church family that afternoon. Those cushioned wooden pews (they had fancier pews in town) were filled with the likes of Hazel, Patty, Paul, Ruth, and Ola Noah (that was her actual last name, although I always got it confused, calling her "Ola Moses").

I've thought about what it meant for me to accept Christ and be baptized at such a young age. I obviously hadn't committed any major sins in my life. Still, I can recognize a few changes that started happening for me right away. It became easier to pay attention during the service. That's what I point to most often when thinking about how becoming a Christian changed me. A few years later, I would become an avid sermon note-taker.

I believe my salvation experience started to change my attitude at school, at home, and in extracurricular activities as well. As the Holy Spirit took up residence in my heart, my actions increasingly exhibited the fruit of the Spirit. Although I don't remember a lot of specifics, I trust God brought more love, joy, peace, patience, kindness, goodness, faithfulness, gentleness, and self-control into my life.

Meet Colleen

She was the first blogger I met in real life, and in my eyes, she was famous. When I first set up my website, tracesoffaith.com, I asked Colleen for help. We sat at a local coffee shop for a few hours one morning, and I left with a website domain and the beginning stages of a blog design. I'm grateful for her. She begins her story:

> When I was young, I looked forward to communion Sunday at the small church my father pastored. Not because it was an opportunity for holy reverence and worship, but because for me it meant extra feasting. My mother, as the wife of a small church pastor, was automatically volunteered for hundreds of different duties. It's similar to being First Lady, only less glamorous and with more organ music. Thus, my mother was tasked with purchasing the grape juice and baking the communion bread. Many Saturdays I helped her. Maybe you have always believed the Lord's Supper is a solemn and sacred event. Little did you know your communion bread was mixed together by a five-year-old wearing a princess costume. Remember, Jesus loves the little children.

What a blessing for a child to be so familiar with the inner workings of the church. My mom cleaned a couple of country churches near our home over the years, and I used to go with her and play Sunday school. Reading about Colleen's time baking communion bread brought back a lot of my own memories. Oh Lord, how I want my daughter to have that same kind of familiarity with the church.

After the unleavened dough was kneaded and rolled flat, my mother stretched it onto a pizza pan and scored it into half inch squares. Then I pricked the dough all over with a fork. Transubstantiation was not a part of our church's doctrine, but admittedly, it does now seem a bit sacrilegious to me that we baked communion bread on a pizza pan.

There was always dough left over. My father's salary at this small church was not substantial, so we were frugal. Nothing went to waste. We baked the extra dough into long strips, topping it with melted butter, sugar, and cinnamon. That was our Saturday night snack while watching *Barbara Mandrell and the Mandrell Sisters*. Again, looking back, this too seems theologically questionable to me.

On Sunday mornings when my father served the Lord's Supper, we walked from the parsonage to the church earlier than usual. My mother carried a green Tupperware bowl filled with the squares of bread we had broken apart after they cooled. In the back of a Sunday school room, I watched my parents fill tiny plastic cups with grape juice, placing each one carefully in the gleaming silver tray. It only took half a bottle of the juice to fill enough cups for our congregation.

I was five years old the first time I took communion. In our church, the only requirement was that you knew Jesus as your Savior. In those early years, I spent a lot of time concentrating on not baptizing my skirt with spilled grape juice and far less time contemplating the complete work of Jesus Christ on the cross. Even now, I fear dropping the communion tray as I gingerly pass it to my pew mate.

> There was always bread left over, and it went home with us, along with the juice. My mother's homemade communion bread was buttery, flaky, and far more flavorful than the Styrofoam wafers churches use today; that stuff is sacrilegious. So, after I survived those harrowing minutes trying not to stain the pew cushions and hymnals, I got to enjoy one of the perks of being a pastor's kid. I spent the afternoons of communion Sunday snacking on the tiny squares of homemade manna. I washed them down with a glass of sweet, purple grape juice. Usually I did so while reading the comics in the Sunday paper. Calvin and Hobbes is philosophically religious, after all.
>
> Now that I'm older, I know my mother made the bread and bought the juice with money from our small household budget, because our church's budget was small as well. I recognize it as her own personal act of worship and communion. An act of which I was a fortunate participant and beneficiary, just as I'm blessed to participate in the Lord's Supper and savor the benefits of God's grace. Today when that plate of wafers comes around, I try not to get distracted. However, I sometimes find myself pondering one very important question: Why do communion bread manufacturers think Jesus tastes like packing peanuts?

After my baptism, I too began taking the Lord's Supper with my church family. Once a quarter, the platters of dry wafers (I've received broken saltine crackers at other churches) and miniature plastic cups of grape juice were placed on a table at the front of the center aisle. After the sermon, there would be special music, and men of the church would come forward and start passing the two trays up and down the aisles. Just like Colleen, I too had a tendency to wiggle, and I would worry my dress would get grape juice on it.

When we started attending our current church, I began taking communion a new way. We take it on the third Sunday of every month, and we receive the elements in a process called intinction, so named for the practice of dipping bread into the cup. This means we go forward and receive the symbolic bread and wine from a church elder who often calls us by name before uttering the timeless, familiar words over each one of us in turn: "This body broken for you . . . This blood spilled out for you." Walking forward to receive, having a blessing of sorts spoken over me as I dip the bread into the juice—this sacrament is now much more meaningful to me. I've learned about churches whose primary focus is on the communion table, with that sacrament being the focal point of every service. Many Episcopal and Anglican churches have the communion table set up in the center of the room. Certainly, the older I get, the more precious that time of communion is to me. Many a Sunday, I could step into a church, receive the bread and wine from a priest or another brother or sister in Christ, cross myself, spend a moment or two in prayer at the altar, and go home completely renewed.

Meet Ronne

I met her a few years ago and found her words online, as she shared about her mission travels worldwide. Mission work has done a mighty work in her heart and she radiates Jesus. A while back, I asked my friends on Facebook how many denominations they had been a part of in their lifetime. If there had been a prize given for the most variety, Ronne would have been in the running.

> Methodist as a very small child. Vagabond girl, attending church with whoever would give me a ride as a child: Baptist, Church of Christ, Assembly of God, Presbyterian, Catholic. Lutheran in high school. Nondenominational when I fully embraced Christ. Followed by hyper-charismatic. Followed by nothing for a while. Then Dutch Reform, and back to nondenominational. Currently enjoying a tiny Episcopal church in the country.

Can you sense the spiritual unrest she's experienced? While I was spending Sunday after Sunday in one church as a child, Ronne was catching rides when she could, visiting whatever church a particular family happened to be attending. I'm confident God used all of these church experiences in Ronne's life to equip her to embrace children around the world who are worshiping Jesus in unique ways. I asked Ronne to describe her communion experience in the Episcopal church she attends now.

> At the beginning of each service at the tiny Episcopal church I call home, Father Paul says, "You are welcome here, and you can't mess this up."
>
> Those words are like potato soup and cornbread and a crackling fire on a chilly winter's evening. They are comforting, nurturing, encouraging. And he's right. Outside of not knowing the exact melody of a song, I've never felt like an outsider. There's a rhythm to the service that carries everyone along, from psalms and prayers read responsively to spoken (and unspoken) prayers.
>
> Communion is a central act of worship at our church. It's an every-week, without-fail thing, like the thoughtful sermons and everyone holding hands while we say the Lord's Prayer, and the tray of candles to be lit by those who long, and hope, and pray. It carries its own pattern of forgiveness and confession, of vulnerability as we drink from the chalice and feel the tender broken bread in our hands. It moves us to a common place.
>
> In my life, communion has become far more than Sunday mornings. On Sunday nights as well, we gather, we yield, we receive at the table with good food and drink. It's not a church service we're having. It's family dinner with a motley crew of friends. But honestly, it may look more like the first communion than anything I know. And it keeps us in a common place. All are welcome at the table.

Overall, when I look back at my early years in the church, I'm more thankful than disillusioned. Like all of us, there were teachings I would reconsider later in life. Mom placed a priority on having us attend church every Sunday. She knew it would be impossible to teach us everything she wanted her children to know about faith and community herself, so she turned to the church for help.

I had a conversation with a friend recently, and she was surprised to hear Dad hadn't joined us at church. She asked me if the people at church treated us differently because we didn't attend as a whole family. What I think she meant was whether the church judged us. Looking back, I couldn't think of a single instance when anything was said about Dad not being with us. I don't remember Mom ever complaining or nagging him to join us either. It's just the way it was.

Every Sunday, we received a bulletin with a pretty picture on the outside cover. Inside, on the left, we'd see the order of worship for that morning. The other side had weekly announcements, maybe a thank you note to the church from someone, or perhaps a birth announcement. On the back of the bulletin, one could find contact information, including church leadership names and phone numbers.

Occasionally, we'd have creative pieces typed up and inserted into the bulletins. Here's one I still have in my childhood Bible:

> Last Sunday I voted to close the church—not maliciously but thoughtlessly.
> I voted to close its doors so its witness and testimony would be stopped.
> I voted to close the Bible on the pulpit—the Bible given to us by the blood of martyrs.
> I voted for our minister to stop preaching the truths of the gospel.
> I voted that children no longer be taught the stories of the Bible and the songs of salvation and God's love.
> I voted that the voice of the choir and the congregation be hushed,
> no more to sing the great hymns of the church.
> I voted for every missionary to be called home.
> I voted for the darkness of superstition, the degrading influence of sin,
> the blight of ignorance, and the curse of selfishness.

I could have gone to church last Sunday, but I didn't. I stayed away.
By my laxity and indifference, I voted to close the church.
—Author Unknown

I often wonder where these close-minded, legalistic thoughts came from, because I don't recall any of our pastors standing at the pulpit doling out lists of what you could and couldn't do. Although perhaps they were and it went right over my head, I'm pretty sure I never had a pastor tell us how to vote in upcoming elections. I don't remember anyone telling me I couldn't dance, but when I attended a private Southern Baptist university my freshman year in college, it was right there in the bylaws. No dancing on campus. No one ever told me I couldn't drink once I was of legal drinking age; however, somewhere along the way I determined it was a major sin. Smoking, being Catholic—it was all forbidden. I just don't remember who told me so.

Most of us can look back at our childhood in the church and realize some legalistic teachings. I think about this now in raising our daughter. She enjoys making her own books. She'll take several pages of clean, white print paper (scrap paper doesn't make good books apparently), fold them in half and staple the book at the sides. A while back, she had made one of her creations and was reading it to me. There was a page where she said if you take the Lord's name in vain (she used to say "take the Lord's name insane" for years, but no longer), you'd go to hell. I think my jaw actually dropped open. She had not learned this theological nugget from her parents. I quickly corrected her and asked her to tell me how we can know we're going to heaven, regardless of our behavior. Jesus is our Savior.

Much of my childhood theology was developed at the week-long vacation Bible schools we'd attend each summer. Back then, VBS was held during the day. It always started outside our church. Promptly at eight we'd have an opening ceremony, starting with three pledges; to the United States flag, the Christian flag, and the Bible. As a kid, you always wanted to be chosen to carry the flags or the Bible into church because you'd get to stand up front. Those flags were heavy, though. I don't remember one ever being dropped, which is probably a miracle in itself. After each pledge, we'd sing a song. Usually "God Bless America," "Onward Christian Soldiers," and "The B-I-B-L-E."

In the churches I'm a part of now, we don't say those pledges anymore. It's rare to see a United States flag in a sanctuary; maybe on Memorial Day Sunday? Veteran's Day? I think separating allegiance to America and Christ's church is wise for the most part. Acknowledging the service of military men and women shows respect, but the Christian flag, the Bible—those are part of a worldwide church. Looking back, I could have benefited from a greater emphasis on that.

Although I would have called my church family our friends, we didn't have families from church over to socialize. Dad wouldn't have known most of them and Mom wouldn't have wanted to make anyone uncomfortable. However, they knew Dad worked for a couple of railroad companies. He'd often be on the road for a week at a time, returning home for Saturday and Sunday. The railroad had its ups and downs financially and Dad would get laid off for long stretches of time. Money got tight and in addition to that, he never seemed to know what to do with himself when he wasn't working.

One winter, Dad was laid off for several months. Mom had part-time work but we didn't have much money. It was an evening in the middle of the week when a few visitors stopped by. I don't recall who it was, but I know they came from our church. They brought a big box full of canned goods. I'm not sure how much we needed that food; Mom never let on, but that incident settled deep down in my soul. If you come up against hard times, the church will help.

I already mentioned Mom never let us miss church on Sunday morning, even on the days when we had plans to go to my grandparents' for lunch (a forty-minute drive one way). As for Sunday evenings, although I'm sure Mom would have liked to attend services; if Dad was around, she stayed home with him. She'd probably watch some TV show she'd rather not be watching, but she did it for her marriage. Dad wasn't going to attend church with her but she wanted to honor their partnership. That meant spending time together when they weren't at work. As a wife, I respect her decision. Back then, I only knew I wanted to go to Sunday night church, so Mary Emma took me. Sunday night service was more relaxed, an even smaller group than on Sunday mornings. We'd sing a few hymns, and then the preacher would lead a topical study or take us through a book of the Bible verse by verse.

As kids, my brothers and I were in a 4-H club, the Springhill Go-Getters, which met monthly in a little one-room building not far from our house or church. Every year our club would have 4-H Sunday. A lot of kids from Mt. Pleasant were in the same 4-H club, so club members often ended up at our church. I also remember visiting Mt. Olive for these services. One 4-H family was Catholic and it seems like we went to Mass for 4-H Sunday a time or two. I don't remember much about it if we did. I was always taught, though I'm not sure by whom, that Catholics worshiped differently than other believers. They hosted big drinking parties at the Knights of Columbus Hall and worshiped Mary. It's quite possible if we did 4-H Sunday at the Catholic church, I would have skipped that Sunday, attending my own church instead.

It wasn't on Mom's radar to give us a variety of church experiences. Many parents don't focus on this. For her, it was enough that we regularly attended our local church. As a child, any additional church activities I participated in were strictly within evangelical churches.

Today, when sharing stories about my spiritual wanderings with my mom, she always advises me to proceed with caution. I visited her a few years back and one morning I sat down with my Bible, a cup of coffee, and a prayer book. It was one I had just gotten, Phyllis Tickle's *The Divine Hours Pocket Edition*. In the morning reading it asked the reader to pray the Gloria. I didn't know what that was. I googled it and wrote the prayer in the back of my book. Sitting beside her on the couch, I mentioned all this to her. She said, "Please be careful. Make sure you're reading something that agrees with the Bible." The opening line of the Gloria is taken from Luke 2:14.

Glory to God in the highest,
and peace to God's people on earth.
Lord God, heavenly King,
almighty God and Father,
we worship you, we give you thanks;
we praise you for your glory.
Lord Jesus Christ, only Son of the Father,
Lord God, Lamb of God,
you take away the sin of the world:
have mercy on us;
you are seated at the right hand of the Father:
receive our prayer.
For you alone are the Holy one,
you alone are the Lord,
you alone are the Most High,
Jesus Christ, with the Holy Spirit,
in the glory of God the Father. Amen

As a mother myself, I do focus on giving my daughter other church experiences. It's important to me she knows there are a variety of ways to worship Jesus. Some seem more solemn, some familiar to the style of her own church, and others will surprise her with charismatic energy. My prayer is God will expand her understanding of Jesus more and more through church experiences I didn't have until much later in life.

I began Bible drills at Calvary Baptist Church my fourth-grade year. The Sunday school board of the Southern Baptist Convention prepared a set of pamphlets with certain memory verses and scripture passages (for instance, the Sermon on the Mount found in Matthew 5-7) for kids to memorize. We also learned the books of the Bible. After we worked on the material in the pamphlet for most of the school year, there was a local competition, followed by an associational one. If you scored high enough there, you moved on to the state level of competition. Ours took place in late spring at Camp Windermere Baptist Assembly. It was fun when you earned that trip because you got to spend the night about three hours away from home for the weekend. They had a cool cave right on the property and we always went there first thing. A natural student, I liked the work of learning the Bible drills material. Even still, I can recall a good portion of what I learned. Verses I memorized then come to me much more readily than those I try to commit to memory today.

"A soft answer turneth away wrath, but grievous words stir up anger." (Proverbs 15:1, KJV) I remember reciting this one as a mantra during my school years. I found it worked quite well for me on the playground.

"So God created man in his own image, in the image of God created he him, male and female created he them." (Genesis 1:27 KJV) A tongue twister if there ever was one. We'd have contests to see who could say it the fastest without messing up.

In elementary school, I attended a weeklong church camp at Grand Oaks Baptist Assembly, about five miles from my house. For a number of years, the camp pastor was Chuck, my former pastor. His family would come and visit camp in the evenings and I enjoyed reconnecting with them again. So many of my childhood church memories include Chuck. Once I met my husband, he graciously let me ask Chuck to perform our wedding ceremony even though they had never met. I can see how God, in all his goodness, found a way for Chuck to be a strong mentor in my faith even after he left Mt. Pleasant. Since my dad didn't play a role in my faith development, I'm thankful for the influence Christian men like Chuck have had on developing my character.

I looked forward to that week at Grand Oaks every summer. Singing all the camp songs, drinking ice cold Nehi peach soda from the snack shop, and swimming were always favorite activities among the campers. If the weather cooperated, we'd have an outdoor service the last night of camp. The speaker would lay out the "plan of salvation," always with a sense of urgency. "If you died tonight, do you know you'd go to heaven?" I had several friends who were saved during our weeks at camp. I'm not going to question the effectiveness of this. There was a lot of emotion surrounding these evenings, which led me to rededicate my life to Christ pretty much every summer. I will say I hope the majority of the decisions were sincere. I like to think those kids went home and told their parents about their decision. Hopefully, they had other adults who continued to teach them about being a Christian. The sanctification process looks different for all of us. I have friends who were born into Christian homes, baptized as infants, and raised in the church. They don't recall a point where they made a salvation decision. That's okay. The important thing is evidence of salvation. For me, the sanctification process was made official at seven years of age. For my daughter, it was when our pastor baptized her at fifteen months old, acknowledging the covenant promises God has made to her and all of us.

The details of our childhood faith experiences can leave us with a lot of questions, but I know this for sure: When I sang the words among those hundreds of other campers—"Shine, Jesus, shine; fill this land with the Father's glory. Blaze, Spirit, blaze; set our hearts on fire"—I meant them. I still do. I'm thankful for camps like Grand Oaks, Camp Windermere and later in my youth, Super Summer and Centrifuge, for helping local churches teach kids that following the ways of Jesus are not only worthwhile, they can also be fun.

Eventually, our church went through another pastoral change. We let Pastor Mike go and welcomed Pastor Gene into our fold. As a tween, it was again hard to understand. Actually, now as an adult, it still doesn't make a lot of sense. It seemed like every time we started to grow and thrive as a church, certain people got uncomfortable. There was a constant tension between moving along with the times and keeping things as they'd always been.

We liked Pastor Gene right away. He and his wife, Wyvonna, owned a Christian bookstore in a nearby town, and they drove round trip an hour-and-a-half to have church with us throughout the week. They hadn't been with us very long when a man who worked for our pastor's bookstore started attending church with his family. It seemed a little strange they would make the long commute to attend our church each Sunday but he and his family seemed to have a lot of respect for our pastor, so we accepted them, of course.

After a month or so, we didn't see the couple at church anymore. The details of the story unfolded slowly piece by piece, because we lived so far from the bookstore and it wasn't something our pastor talked about openly. The husband had apparently been stealing money from our pastor's store for a while. We never saw them again and I never heard the exact amount he stole. What I did hear though, loud and clear, was this—our pastor refused to press charges. He was a man called by God and chose not to pursue what was rightfully his through the justice system. He forgave the man for everything he had done, they cut ties, and that was the end of it. Pastor Gene's decision was an amazing act of grace done in complete humility.

I often wonder how things would have been different if we'd stayed at Mt. Pleasant. The pastors would come and go, but know this; Jesus never left. He might have been frustrated with us at times, but he was in the midst of our mess—he always is.

Meet Donnie

> I was raised and baptized as a Baptist. My family being from the south, it was our religion of choice. My grandmother, Daisy, was the strong religious presence of my family.
>
> My mother and father rarely if ever went to church. Maybe on Mother's Day or Easter but I cannot remember a time, when I was a child, that my mother and father went to church with me, my siblings, and my grandmother. Later in life, when we were grown, both my mother and father returned to the church before they passed away.
>
> My grandmother had me and my siblings in church at least three times a week and twice on Sundays. I remember numerous times the preacher of our church came to my grandmother's house for Sunday dinner, and my siblings and I had to wait until he had eaten before we could eat. There were no feelings of animosity; it's just the way it was. We all knew that my grandmother was deeply religious and the preacher was held in high esteem in her house.

As a child, until I went away to boarding school in New Hampshire, I went to church with my grandmother. In 1969, after arriving at my new school, the first thing I did was go to the only church in town. It was the first time that I, an African American, from the ghetto of Chicago, attended an all-white church. At first it was a little uncomfortable because it wasn't the fiery sermon that I had become accustomed to from the eloquent Baptist preacher back home. However, I knew I had to be in church because that was what my grandmother had instilled in me.

In 1973, after high school, I joined the Air Force. In basic training, I went to church every Sunday because it allowed us to get out of the barracks for a couple of hours. A few years later, I was married with twins on the way, and my new wife was not a church person so I strayed from the church. I always prayed but I stopped attending church. As a matter of fact, it wasn't until 1981, when I became a Chicago police officer, that I started thinking about church again. No, I didn't go, but it was always in the back of my mind.

In 1985 I got shot and went on disability with the police department. I moved to a new suburban town and began attending a Church of God in Christ church with a therapist from the North Chicago VA hospital. I was not connected to this church and I was just going through the motions of organized religion while there.

In 1990, I divorced my first wife. I met my second wife that I have been married to for twenty-seven years now and she is a cradle Episcopalian. I went to church with her a couple of times when we were dating, but I wasn't feeling the Episcopal church. I guess it was because the church we went to at the time was high church, with all of the pomp and circumstance. I didn't know about high church, so I thought all Episcopal churches were like this one.

In 1994, my wife and I moved to Downers Grove and we started attending an Episcopal church with her mother. This church wasn't at all like the one in Chicago and I felt a little better about it. However, I also started going to the Baptist church, with my wife's sister and her husband. I would alternate between churches because I felt going to an Episcopal church was somehow betraying my grandmother.

I continued to go to the Episcopal church with my wife and her mother. However, I also went to the Baptist church there until my sister-in-law and her husband divorced. I then started going to the Episcopal church full-time but not every Sunday.

On December 9, 2009, I was driving home from a Christmas party in Chicago given by my Masonic lodge. I had too much to drink and I remember waking up on a frontage road with no recollection of how I got off the expressway. Then I realized that I had crashed into a light post and my car was totaled. My eye and chest hurt. My first thought was, "God, please don't let it be that I have killed someone." Fortunately for me, I just wrecked a fence, a light post, and my car.

I received a DUI, community service, and restitution for the fence and light post. While deciding where to perform community service, I knew it had to be with the church. I had gone to St. Benedict Episcopal Church, and I remembered that the vicar there, Reverend Heidi, had preached a good sermon the couple of times I had gone there. I decided that if she would let me, I would do my community service at St. Benedict.

Reverend Heidi gave me odd jobs to do around the church, painting mostly. I decided that since I was doing community service at St. Benedict, I would attend services and sit in the back and just listen. Little did I know that God and Reverend Heidi had other plans for me.

Little by little, Reverend Heidi worked her "Jedi mind trick" on me and I found myself doing more than just listening. I never had any intentions of being active in the church, other than coming and dropping a few dollars in the basket during the offering.

However, the congregation of St. Benedict was so hospitable and welcoming that I began to feel very comfortable and I knew I was supposed to be at this church. I began participating in church functions, I attended an Inquirers' class and I got confirmed into the Episcopal church. I was elected to the Bishop's Committee and became a warden for two years. I have been on discernment groups for members answering God's call.

I was a co-chair for a selection committee for a new priest for St. Benedict, and I continue today as one of the leaders of this church. I never came to this church looking to be a leader; I just wanted to do my community service and continue with my life as it had been, but now I know that God's plan for me is so much greater than I could have ever imagined.

I have attended the Chicago diocesan convention since 2010, serving as a lay delegate numerous times. I am a member of the Chicago diocese congregations committee, serving as a liaison for three Episcopal churches in the diocese. I am a member of a "Grace and Race" ministry at St. Benedict and my faith is as strong, if not stronger, as it was when I was a child, while attending New Covenant Baptist Church with my grandmother.

I've been in church for forty-plus years. Don't think for a minute it's always easy or there aren't times when hefty doses of grace and forgiveness are needed, yet I've never considered leaving the church. I watched my dad live a life without the church and I didn't want any part of that. Generations of my biological family have faithfully attended church, and I know I have a place in that heritage.

If you're in the church long enough it will disappoint you, I promise. The way I always saw it, disappointment left me with choices. I could stick it out and try to make a positive change in the church I attended. I could determine the fellowship was broken enough I needed to find a new church home. Or I could ultimately decide God was to blame for the hurt and suffering, causing me to abandon church altogether. This last choice never seemed a viable option to me.

Chapter 2

Storm-Tossed

Eventually, the rumors at church started up again. We'd have a guest preacher or two all of a sudden. Then special business meetings attended by lots of people, including "members" who rarely participated on Sunday mornings. I was older this time around and understood what was going on a bit more. Not that it ever made sense.

Some people in the church wanted to get rid of Pastor Gene. The humble, genteel man we'd grown to love over the past few years. There was nothing we could do to stop it. The people who wanted our pastor gone always seemed to get the votes they needed. In the twelve years we attended that church, we said hello and goodbye to three pastors. That's once every four years if you're doing the math. Not allowing for the in-between times when another pastoral committee would be formed, and we'd hear from interim pastors. It left us in an exhausting cycle of spiritual upheaval.

I learned many lessons from this experience. The primary one is that most of the time church offers a sweet fellowship, and the majority of people are there to worship Jesus and do good. Then, there's the political side. Church as a business. At times a power hungry side that gets ugly fast. I also learned that even though fellowship might feel broken, we're still under the lordship of Christ. Church family is still family, even when we don't get along.

I talked with Mom about this part of my church story recently. She mentioned something I don't recall hearing before. She spoke with Pastor Gene one of his last few Sundays at church. He expressed regret over never meeting my dad. "I really think I could have connected with him," he said. "Maybe got him to start coming to church."

Pastor Gene resigned. In the interim, we had a few men take the pulpit as guests. There was talk of another search committee. Ultimately, I did know of the man they hired for their next pastor because his kids started attending my school. However, he was never my family's pastor. We talked it over, and together we decided to transfer our church membership.

It was an agonizing decision. In all my days since, I'm not able to casually attend a church. When I find a church home, I'm all in from the moment I first become involved. I have left a number of churches for various reasons over the years, but it has never again been due to a church split. I would later learn another term for my allegiance to a local church. Covenant relationship, a deliberate and mutual commitment to Christ and a particular body of believers through our participation in a local church. It seems to be lost terminology in most of our congregations.

For my family, the question then became where we were going to go. This time, when we let our preacher go, it became a true church split. Several families were hurt and decided to find a new church home. Many of them moved to another country church. We were hesitant to take that route again. Who's to say another group of church members wouldn't form an alliance and start kicking out pastors like we'd already experienced? We wanted a bigger organization, hopefully with a few more checks and balances regarding the business side of the church.

What if finding another church is difficult and takes a long time? Will the next church be better? How do we choose to make a change and take that leap of faith for another community to become our community? What if church is your entire community, your way of life? In considering church stories that weren't like mine, a friend suggested I talk with Crystal. She grew up Amish, but when things got especially hard in their family, they couldn't stay.

Meet Crystal

I grew up in the Amish church. Churches consist of a district, which includes one bishop, two preachers, and a deacon. The bishop is considered the leader, the one who makes final decisions. Sunday church starts around nine a.m. and ends around noon, and then you have lunch together. They have bread, peanut butter spread, cheese spread, jam and butter, and a few varieties of cookies. I always enjoyed this time because it was so delicious. Church itself, for me, was more like a three-hour sitting period. I didn't understand when preachers read out of the Bible, because it was read in German. In my Amish district, we didn't have a church house. Each person in that district took turns servicing church at their house. They also had church every other Sunday, so they could have the opportunity to visit churches in nearby districts. I remember whenever my aunts or uncles had church at their house, we would go. This is probably the only time I enjoyed going to church because I got to play with my cousins.

What district (church) you are in depends on where you live. You are to follow the rules of that district. If they are broken, you must go in front of the church to confess your "sin." I put this in quotation because it's not always what God would consider a sin, but what the Amish consider a sin based on their rules. If you don't confess your sin publicly, you will be shunned. Shunning consists of not allowing one to participate in communion, washing of the feet, or participating in the church (which includes voting, cooking, and other activities). My mom was shunned from the Amish church. It all started when my dad left. The bishops and preachers blamed everything on my mom. About the same time, my brother decided he wanted to attend high school. The Amish only go through eight years of schooling, so high school was frowned upon. My mom told our church leadership my brother wanted to go through high school to avoid *Rumspringa*, a period of running around when an individual turns sixteen. It's a time to experience the English world, and can include lots of partying. Not every Amish teen takes part in this, but it is allowed if they choose to do so. The bishop thought this was a better idea than high school because "that's the way we do things." Later, I would go through *Rumspringa*. I made some terrible decisions, none that I am proud of, yet none that I regret.

After experiencing such outright rejection from the Amish church, I began going with my uncle to his church, the First Church of God. This was the beginning of my faith. My family stayed with the Amish community until after my sister got married, out of respect for her, even though my mom was shunned at the wedding and didn't get to help with anything. Eventually, we ended up attending an English church. My mom is still shunned by the Amish, although my younger siblings and I are not shunned because we never officially joined the Amish church through baptism. The fact that my older sister remained Amish and the rest of us are not hasn't changed our relationship at all. We are super close as a family and do not pay much attention to each other's way of life. We are focused on our love for one another, not our clothes or lifestyle. The Missionary church where we initially settled after leaving the Amish community is where I was finally baptized. It's been five years now, and I haven't looked back. That church ended up closing though. We didn't know where to go, still being new in our faith. I remembered going to the First Church of God with my uncle, and suggested we try there. My family and I have been there ever since, and enjoy it. I do not miss a single thing about my life as an Amish girl. I do want to express that this was in one district of the Amish church. Other Amish families will have different experiences. Today, I am so happy and joyful. I have found true freedom and real, pure love. The only love.

I appreciate Crystal's story because her unfortunate circumstances didn't stop her from pursuing Jesus. Or rather, he didn't stop pursuing her. She found churches that welcomed her and her family, and she's thriving in her faith today. Crystal's story brings up an important point though. For every person we meet who has a good church experience, there are others who struggle, sometimes mightily.

There was a woman who started attending my Bible study. She warmed up to our group right away and, as a new Christian, she blossomed. She hadn't grown up in church and as God revealed himself to her through his word, she grew hungry for more. At one point she stopped coming. First one week, then two. Eventually I heard her husband had found a girlfriend at work. The marriage fell apart. She stopped attending our Bible study and I reached out one on one but she'd rarely respond. Eventually she did start sharing more details. Divorce, child support, heated discussions over custody. It was the hardest season of her life. Not only did she stop attending Bible study, for a long time she didn't go to church. Our group supported her but she carried a lot of shame. She'd been doing everything right, walking this new path with Jesus. Why did this happen to her? How could she face the church again? Several of us stayed beside her, meeting for coffee and exchanging conversations over the phone. We prayed. Over time she has healed. A few years ago she met someone new and they got married, at our home. It was a beautiful tale of redemption. Although she attends another church now, she visits ours from time to time. It's a blessing for her to do so. This is an example of a church handling divorce with grace. It's a story of a woman who had to leave for a time in order to let Jesus heal her heart.

We need to hear church stories, good and bad, from other people, and hold them in our hands and hearts with tender loving care.

The spring of my sophomore year in high school, we started attending First Baptist Church in town. It was this church that loaned its baptistry to our country church on occasion. Their pastor had been there for almost twenty-five years, which screamed of stability to my family. I already knew several of the kids from going to school with them. This was also the church where Pastor Chuck served as youth pastor. It seemed like as good a place as any for a new beginning.

Compared to the church experiences I was used to, First Baptist seemed huge. The sanctuary seated about five hundred and the pews cushioned in purple fabric seemed luxurious. When I went to Sunday school, I tried to use the same stairs going up to the second floor and back down; otherwise, I would become disoriented. We had really hit the big time.

We went back to Mt. Pleasant one final time. I don't remember what was going on that evening, but we showed up a few minutes before the service was scheduled to start. One of the church's faithful, Hazel, greeted us at the door. She'd hosted my mom's Bible study group at her farmhouse just a few miles from church several times over the years. She rushed up and hugged us all. "Oh, I was so afraid you were leaving, too," she said. While it nearly broke our hearts, we stuck to our decision.

We attended First Baptist for some time before officially joining as members. In the Southern Baptist churches I attended, you moved your letter of membership by walking down the aisle during the invitation hymn at the end of a service. After meeting briefly with a pastor, staff member, or deacon, you filled out a membership form and after the closing prayer, the family would stay up front so those in the church could come and shake your hand, introducing themselves to you.

I knew a handful of people from this new church, but most of the faces were unfamiliar to me at the time. People who eventually became precious to me were strangers at this point. The emotion of it all overwhelmed me and I stood there crying during our entire meet and greet. I'm sure people probably thought I was crazy. Leaving behind the only church I'd ever known, thinking of the church family I'd broken fellowship with, missing all those pastors. It was the close of a chapter of my life, and I had no idea how to end it well.

One woman who had attended Mt. Pleasant sporadically in her younger years approached me toward the end of the receiving line. I guess she thought she knew my situation. With a sense of bewilderment, she asked, "Why are you crying? This should be an exciting day to join our church and start a new chapter."

She would be the first of many to tell me I took this church thing a bit too seriously. I have a difficult time criticizing the church, even when it's deserved. Does God give some people an extra dose of love for the church? And if so, what are we supposed to do with that? These are musings I continue to live into.

I found my place among the youth at First Baptist pretty quickly. Pastor Chuck led an active youth group and I quickly connected with those classmates of mine who had always called First Baptist their home church. Church activities quickly filled up my social calendar. I was at church every time the doors were opened, as the saying goes. That was fine by me.

Becky was my best friend all through high school. She didn't attend my church but the Catholic one across town, St. Columban's. Once I got my driver's license, if I wasn't at home, working, or with my friends from youth group, I was probably at Becky's. I wasn't sure what to expect spending that much time with a Catholic family. A popular TV show at the time, *Just the Ten of Us*, was about a Catholic family who moved to the west coast so the dad could be a high school PE teacher and coach. They had a houseful of kids, a few crosses on their walls, and the mom prayed a lot. I figured my friend's house would be something like that.

Well, I don't remember any crosses on the wall. They did have a lot of kids. Their dad owned and operated a local restaurant. I began waitressing for him some nights and weekends. He asked me once how my tips were coming along. They seemed about average and I told him so. He laughed and said, "Well, just tell the customers you're one of my daughters and you'll get better tips. I have so many, nobody knows who is who anyway."

Even though Becky's family didn't use the same theological language I did, they were Christians. I attended Mass with them a few times. During Mass, they knelt on weird benches, and I learned I couldn't take communion with them. The service was hard to follow, but I always recited the Lord's Prayer when it came along. I recognized passages from scripture. My junior year another friend who was Catholic lost her mom, and I watched the Catholics hold a necklace called a rosary, fingering it in their hand as they recited some prayers. Again, I recognized the Lord's Prayer and something about Mary. I determined Catholics could be Christians after all, even if they drank a little. This may sound silly, but it was revolutionary for me.

Every year, during a period of time Becky's family called Lent, the kids gave up things like Dr. Pepper, chocolate, or bubble gum. I know now Lent is a season of the liturgical church calendar when Christians focus on the forty days Jesus spent being tempted by Satan in the wilderness before he started his earthly ministry. People often give something up or take on a new practice during this time as a way of focusing on their relationship with God, preparing their hearts for Easter. We'd also order Casey's Pizza on those Friday nights, topped with cheese only because Catholics give up eating meat on the Fridays of Lent. These practices were entirely new to me. I had no idea why they did these things and I never thought to ask.

How often I have longed to relive those high school days, hanging out with this family. I could have learned so much from their Catholic-ness. The rhythm of aligning daily lives with the church calendar. Knowledge about the saints. Exactly what is purgatory? I would have pelted them with questions. The very questions I've spent the last ten years of my life trying to answer for myself.

There were other churches in my hometown I didn't attend because I had misgivings about how they worshiped. I don't know if I would have gone so far to say they were wrong, but they certainly left me nervous. The Church of Christ didn't believe in playing instruments during praise and worship. They baptized a person the moment he or she made a profession of faith. Cornerstone Church, on the edge of town, was a nondenominational charismatic church where they rolled in the aisles and spoke in tongues. Surely a person couldn't find an authentic relationship with Jesus in places like this. Could they?

As I worked on this book, I knew we needed to hear a charismatic voice. I asked if any of my friends would be willing to share about their experience in this tradition. Reba volunteered. I appreciate her passion for the faith.

Meet Reba

> I was raised in a Pentecostal home and church and have always attended one. Even to this day. I remember praying at the altar growing up. I remember late-night revival services. I was baptized in seventh grade and baptized again as a senior. I wanted to rededicate my life to Christ after having a few rebellious teenage years. I've sat in church services and been so overwhelmed by his presence that all I could do was cry. Sometimes I feel his presence so strongly that it makes my hands shake. It wasn't fake. It was real. It's not something I can really explain. He's never spoken to me audibly, but I have heard him speak to my spirit, and I've known when I've needed to go pray for people. I believe in all of the gifts of the Spirit. I believe in the Holy Spirit and speaking in tongues. I have spoken in tongues several times in my own life. Nothing loud or service-interrupting, but in my personal prayer time at the altar. I do not know how to explain it, I just know it's real. The joy and peace I have with his Spirit is real. I do believe people can get caught up in emotionalism or not treat the gifts correctly. Things can get out of hand. I have also witnessed that first hand. But the real presence of God is so amazing and something I always want to experience.
>
> We raise our hands in worship during our worship services. It is a sign of surrender and worship and awe to our king. Sometimes people may kneel or jump during a faster song. It's all to show our love to him. We go to concerts and sporting games and jump and clap and shout so why not in celebration of him and his salvation? He saved my soul from hell and I'm so thankful he did.

> I believe in anointing with oil and the laying on of hands. I have experienced his healing in my life. I dealt with anxiety and panic attacks for about a year of my life and was anointed and prayed for several times. I also had my house anointed with oil and had a prayer cloth I carried in my purse. God healed me and I am medication free today.

I don't know much about the charismatic tradition. It didn't fit with my conservative upbringing and I have heard stories of these acts of worship being abused. Still, every time I read those 28 chapters in Acts, I wonder if I'm experiencing all of God that I can. He's real in my life, but is he mighty? Reba continues:

> We participate in the Lord's Supper quarterly at our church. Everyone who is a Christian can participate, whether you are a member or not. I read my Bible throughout the week. I can't say I do this daily, but I try. I have also led a few women's Bible studies in my church. God is always revealing himself to me as I read. I hunger to hear from him and to learn and grow closer to him. I read from several different versions but my favorite is the English Standard Version. It's easy to understand and brings scripture to light. I love reading different versions to understand a passage more.
>
> As a child, it was honestly embarrassing at times to be in church. I didn't understand the importance of the energy. Part of my discomfort was because things were done out of order. Now that I'm an adult and have a pastor who doesn't let things get out of hand, I understand and I love it. Order truly makes all the difference. The Holy Spirit is a gentleman, and is not the author of chaos and confusion, so you must have balance in the Pentecostal tradition.

In high school, a new family moved to our small town and the husband became my Sunday school teacher. Greg was a great Bible teacher. He had a wealth of knowledge and did a good job including everyone in class discussions. Greg's wife, Donna, partnered with him in leading our class and offered excellent insight. Her real strength, though, was in making sure everyone felt welcome. She took the time to learn about each one of us and would then remember to check in about what she'd learned. Looking at Donna, I can tell you what a sister in Christ should look like.

Greg never shied away from the hard questions of our faith. No theological discussion was off limits to him. To this day, when I run up against a theological wall, Greg takes time out of his own busy life to schedule a phone call and examine my questions with me. He's recommended dozens of books to me over the years, perhaps none more significant to both of us than Lauren Winner's *Girl Meets God.* Her description of lifelong friendships expresses our relationship with Greg and Donna's family perfectly:

> There are a few people out there with whom you fit just so, and, amazingly, you keep fitting just so even after you have growth spurts or lose weight or stop wearing high heels. You keep fitting after you have children or change religions or stop dyeing your hair or quit your job at Goldman Sachs and take up farming. Somehow, God is gracious enough to give us a few of these people, people you can stretch into, people who don't go away, and whom you wouldn't want to go away, even if they offered to.

Our families have vacationed together, mostly camping. I remember one year in particular, Greg shared a disagreement he was having with someone at church. The person decided he didn't want to be in close fellowship with Greg anymore. It left Greg reeling and ended up being a hurtful situation. So damaging, in fact, Greg considered leaving the only church they'd attended since moving to town. Greg did a lot of soul searching in that time and that's when he stumbled across Winner's book. It helped him examine his own faith and establish what he really believed.

After continuing to struggle with the broken relationship with this brother in Christ, Greg visited the local Episcopal church one particular afternoon (Winner is an Episcopalian). He sat down with the priest to learn more about this small church in my hometown. The priest asked Greg a number of questions about his church experience. He inquired about how Greg's wife and daughters felt about their church family. Apparently a very wise priest, he spent most of the conversation listening to Greg's reflections. After a time, he offered Greg this advice, "Some people look their whole lives to find a church experience like you've described to me. It sounds like it has been a huge blessing to you and your family. My advice is stay right where you are."

That story taught me a valuable lesson. You're not going to find the perfect church experience. In fact, the more involved you get, you're sure to find flaws in these all-too-human establishments. Yet the local church is where Christ chooses to do his work on this earth, through the Holy Spirit who lives in the body of believers as a whole. It shouldn't be easy to break a covenant relationship you've made with fellow Christ-followers. Are there times people should consider leaving? Absolutely, but I would hope it's a gut-wrenching decision. If a church splits over a controversy and your fellowship is wounded beyond repair; if your doctrinal stance on a major theological point differs with a current congregation in an undeniable way; if your family is in danger physically, emotionally, or spiritually—these are reasons to consider leaving. For the most part, in my personal experience, we've made it too easy to leave. I often wonder how many good and hard faith conversations we miss out on because one or the other party chooses to leave the church. Think of the message we'd send our children if we rode out the highs and lows a church family will experience in their eighteen years of childhood. Rather than looking for a perfect church, look to meet God in the church you call home.

In another one of our conversations, Greg shared his beliefs regarding drinking alcohol, and how they didn't coincide with Southern Baptist doctrine on the topic. He'd been approached once about being a deacon at our Baptist church. As a deacon he would consider official business that the church would ultimately bring before the entire congregation to vote on. He would also help with congregational visits to the elderly and sick, and help the poor in the community as the church became aware of specific needs. Knowing his views on drinking didn't line up with church doctrine, he decided to turn down the nomination. One of the godliest men I know couldn't serve his church in this capacity (although apparently teaching was fine) over something like having a social drink.

A few years after settling in to First Baptist, I found myself looking for a new church family again, for reasons not so painful this time. As a college freshman, I attended a Southern Baptist University in southern Missouri. It thrilled me to think about all the religiousness I was going to soak up as I left home to pursue a higher education. I had resolved not to be one of those Christians who got a taste of freedom and became a backslider.

For many of us, the young adult years are when we wrestle with making our faith personal. We're not under the instruction of our parents any longer, so we start making our own decisions about attending church, daily time with God, and the people we hang out with socially. As a parent, I view this fast-approaching time in an entirely different way. I spend a lot of time thinking through the tools of faith we're giving our daughter now, while she's still a child. Sure, some of it goes over her head. My bigger concern is what ultimately penetrates her heart. I know many Christians who let Christ and his church take a back seat to other priorities in these formative years. If you feel like this was you, ask God for forgiveness. Trust him to continue revealing himself to you and your children (even the adult ones) in meaningful ways. If, like me, you're a parent in the midst of raising a child in the faith, cover your children in prayer. Let them see you living out an active faith, not just checking "church to-do items" off a list. Finally, realize they will need to forge their own relationship with Jesus. The narrow road may look a little bumpy at times, but God is faithful.

Meet Bailey

When I first started reading Bailey's writing, I discovered she was walking a path much like my own. She hadn't grown up in a tradition of formal liturgy, but when she experienced it as an adult, she found new ways to encounter Jesus that settled deep in her soul. These spiritual disciplines provided healing and comfort when she found herself thousands of miles away from friends and family.

> My church experience has always been focused on my individual church. Fellowship was the highest purpose of Sundays. We gathered with other Christians to develop friendships, to learn, and to worship through singing. I enjoyed church on Sundays but when college arrived, I didn't see the need for it anymore.
>
> You see, I had a personal relationship with God. I went to chapel and Thursday night worship night. My friends in my dorm were all believers and the professors encouraged Christian thought. What more could I need?
>
> My mom questioned once if it bothered me to not take the Lord's Supper. I was confused. Since the Lord's Supper was simply a way to remember Christ's sacrifice, I didn't know why I couldn't remember it on my own, privately. Because, to put it bluntly, communion simply didn't mean much to me.

This is a common mentality among my evangelical friends. Most churches don't serve the Lord's Supper every Sunday, and when they do, trays of bread and grape juice are passed up and down the rows of pews. That's how I received it the first thirty years of my life, and I didn't think much of it. From my own experience, and here in Bailey's story, I wonder if we're doing our congregants a great disservice in limiting their exposure to Christ's table.

> As an adult, that all changed. The first time I took the Lord's Supper in a PCA [Presbyterian Church in America] church, I immediately felt out of place. People were standing up and walking forward as one would do in Mass to receive the elements. I awkwardly stood and fumbled down the aisle. As I tore off a piece of bread the elder looked me in the eye and said, "The body of Christ given for you."

I mumbled a quick thank you, thinking to myself, "as if the body of our Lord was his to offer," reached for a little cup of wine and was met with another elder looking me in the eye and admonishing me with, "The blood of Christ; drink and be blessed."

My view on communion has changed since that first Sunday in the PCA church. I have developed a different theology and I know there are mysteries that, for now, are reserved only for the knowledge of the Lord. Mysteries that look like a small piece of bread and sip of wine, but are so much more. I don't always cry when I partake, but often I am so overwhelmed by grace, the realization makes its way to the corners of my eyes.

Sundays took on a new meaning after that day. Worship became less about learning, less about offering myself through song, and more about receiving what the Lord offered to me. I realized I didn't have anything to offer God. My worship wasn't about singing with the most emotion or learning tips for living out my faith. Suddenly, worship became about tasting the grace of God.

Communion reinvigorated my love for Sabbath worship. There, I found something I couldn't find anywhere else. I held the Lord's sacrifice in my hands and remembered who I was. A sinner. A desperate sinner in need of desperate grace. But I am never left there. I am reminded of my lowly state, but I am lavished with a God who would sacrifice himself on my behalf. As I hold the bread and the wine, I am reminded that I am to go and serve a God who has promised to sustain me with his body and blood. In communion, I hold the world's largest mystery between my fingers. And I now crave this life-giving nourishment.

The majority of the students I met at university my freshman year attended one of two Baptist churches in the small town where the school was located. I joined the ones who attended First Baptist. I'd had a pretty good experience up to now with people at First Baptist churches. There was a girl my age whose dad taught at the university and she'd grown up at the church I was now attending. She knew everyone and the elderly had been there changing her diapers in the beginning. It left me feeling like an outsider. I don't think she set out to be exclusive, but she didn't make an effort to be welcoming either. During this time, I internalized a lesson. There's a certain amount of effort required to make a person feel included. I haven't always gotten this right myself because feeling at home is pretty cozy. My eyes were opened, though. If it's really God's church, everyone belongs there. We need to be intentionally welcoming.

We simply must move beyond our comfort levels. I think of the individuals who aren't comfortable in our congregations, such as those who think their sin is so great they don't dare darken a church door. Yet, as Jesus told us in Mark 2:17, "Those who are well have no need of a physician, but those who are sick; I have come to call not the righteous but sinners." What about those individuals who come to us from foreign soil, not speaking our language or understanding our culture? Or with darker skin? In Austin Channing Brown's book, *I'm Still Here*, she shares about her experience as an African American woman traversing evangelical Christianity. So many times, as I read this book, I felt uncomfortable, because I realized all the ways we as a church leave Austin uncomfortable. I realized again and again, I wanted to know about the Christianity she experienced as a child—in particular, the style of worship she had encountered. What do we miss because we sit comfortably among people just like us Sunday after Sunday?

> The Black church gave me the greatest sense of belonging I had ever experienced. There was still much to learn; speaking in tongues, being slain in the Spirit, prophetic announcements and praise dances. (Not to mention, I hadn't realized that you could be in such a large group and everyone could clap in time on the two and four. Like everyone. . . .) It was an adjustment, but none of this made me nervous or uncomfortable . . . I loved the Black church and she loved me.

I only attended this Baptist university for one year, but it was enlightening. For the first time, I started to realize Baptists could have a lot of rules. I guess I knew that at some level. Because of my religious beliefs, I had never had a drink, wouldn't think of touching a cigarette (or worse), and I believed wholeheartedly in the sanctity of all life. But at this university, I was also told chapel attendance was mandatory, you absolutely should be in church on Sundays, and according to the by-laws, dancing on campus was not allowed. Also, girls weren't ever going to be pastors, and thus had no reason to take Hebrew (I know this because I was the girl who asked if I could take Hebrew *for fun*).

The biggest surprise I encountered during my freshman year occurred socially. One of the reasons I chose to attend a Christian university was so I could encounter Jesus in a bigger way. I envisioned Friday nights doing Bible study, summers taking mission trips, and an overdose of praise and worship every day. If you wanted these things, you could find them, but what I discovered was not everyone was there looking for a richer faith experience. Some of the students attended this university on athletic scholarships, while others were sent there by their parents (occasionally even in an attempt to undo lifestyle choices the parents disapproved of), and others chose this college because it was close to home. It wasn't all Jesus all the time, unless you wanted it to be. I began to learn no one takes more responsibility for your faith walk than you do.

For financial reasons, the following year I moved back home to attend classes at a junior college. I only had one more year of general education left, and had no idea where I'd attend school after that, but for now, I'd come home. It felt good.

Home for me also meant returning to the congregation at First Baptist. My friends from the youth group were, for the most part, away at college so I often attended Sunday School with my grandma. Her Sunday school teacher was Ms. Betty, whose grandson was a dear friend of mine. I knew Ms. Betty to be a spiritual giant. It turns out the older adult women's class reads the same Bible we did in youth group. I felt completely comfortable attending this class. They were happy to have me, smiling from ear to ear when I'd come in with Grandma. Christianity transcends age.

But Wednesdays were my favorite day of the week. Mom was the coordinator for the dinners our church served prior to evening classes and prayer meeting. My Aunt Betty and a friend, Sharon, would join us on Wednesday afternoons to help with the preparations. What a sweet time of fellowship cooking with these women in the church kitchen. At mealtime, I'd collect money as people came in to eat. One elderly man always winked at me and said he was "Mr. Hinkel" when he'd give me his name. He found himself quite funny. I barely remember his actual name; he'll always be Mr. Hinkel to me.

That year, I took two semesters of humanities (philosophy) to fulfill the requirements needed for an associate's degree. We started right out of the gate reading books I would have never read on my own—these weird Greek classics, like *Antigone* and *Oedipus the King*, or French philosopher Albert Camus's *The Stranger*. I went into these classes with my guard up because I'd heard horror stories about how college philosophy classes could warp the minds of decent Christian folk (like me). The professor challenged us to think. He never once questioned my belief in Jesus, but pushed me to identify the world lens my faith gave me, and how that affected my everyday life. I realized, for the first time, my particular form of Christian upbringing influenced every aspect of my life from my politics, to my cultural understandings, to my future plans to have a family. I couldn't undo what I'd learned, but I could hone it. I could learn more. Reading the course material in these classes started me down a path to do that.

I also took a college-level sociology class at the local tech center. The teacher, who attended my church, planned to show a newly released movie, *Philadelphia*. In this movie, a man with HIV, played by Tom Hanks, is fired by his law firm. He hires a small-time lawyer, played by Denzel Washington, to represent him in a wrongful dismissal suit. Washington is the only lawyer willing to take on the case. I struggled mightily deciding whether or not to watch the film. At that point in my theological development, I had lived a sheltered life, and feared watching movies like this might negatively impact my overall conservative worldview. I didn't know a single person who struggled with his or her sexual identity (actually that wasn't true, but I wasn't aware of that yet). It made me uncomfortable to even think about watching a movie on this topic. I told my teacher I wouldn't be attending class that evening, for religious reasons.

In the Gospel of Luke we read a parable Jesus told in response to a lawyer who asked, "And who is my neighbor?" In this story, a man gets robbed by some real professionals, who leave him for dead. Three men happen upon this abandoned man, lying on the road: a priest, a Levite (temple assistant), and a Samaritan. The first two ignore the man entirely. If you asked them why, they'd likely cite religious reasons. Their laws forbid the handling of anything unclean. The Samaritan, sworn enemy of the Jewish people, is the one who sets aside any differences and stops to help. Not only does he check on the man, but he cleans his wounds, bandages him up, and pays for healing time at a nearby inn with his own money. This is certainly above-and-beyond attention.

"Which of these do you think was a neighbor to the man?" Jesus asked. The lawyer said, "The one who showed him mercy." We cannot overlook that message. Jesus calls us to be good neighbors. Religious reasoning can get in the way of mercy.

Over the years, I've had a handful of close childhood friends "come out of the closet." One such friend has been married for a while and she and her wife have a son. Together, they are raising him in the Jewish faith and it's been beautiful to see her find healing and peace after her own hard childhood. When they announced the birth of their son, I knew just what I wanted to give them, a wooden Shabbat set. It thrills me to see their little boy wearing a yarmulke on his head, using his wooden set of dishes, every time she shares Sabbath photos with me.

Then there are the people I have never met face to face but interact with on social media. In the Gospel of Matthew, we're told that Christ-followers are known by their fruit. Time and again, I see good and godly fruit from gay and lesbian friends I know online. They are teaching me things about Jesus, his deep love for all people, and his scandalous grace that embraces all who will accept it.

My gay and lesbian friends are precious to me. I'm still developing a context where my beliefs can coincide with my love for these friends. The love Jesus absolutely calls us to—but what does that look like in our homes, our churches, and around our communities?

Meet Leslie

The list of things that can divide us is long. I knew I wanted to include a story from someone who has benefited from ecumenical (representing a number of different churches) interaction. I found Leslie through a Facebook writing group, in the eleventh hour of this manuscript. She grew up Catholic, but spent her early adult years "wandering," to borrow her term. What she found in her days of exploring was that these churches and traditions all had something to offer her in the ways of Jesus. Although she ultimately went back to her Catholic roots, she has a heart for continuing to build relationships with all Christians. One of the ways she does this is through her participation in a series of ecumenical evangelistic classes available globally.

> Sometimes wandering is good. Wandering affords us a different perspective and the ability to make discoveries.
>
> I was born and raised Catholic, and typical to many in their teen years on into early adulthood, I concluded religion was non-essential. A long period of wandering eventually led me to explore many different churches and traditions. Exploration can be a gift, especially if we bring home some treasured souvenirs from our visit. Exposure to other churches gave me a greater appreciation, realizing God is always in the midst of our gatherings, and if we are open and teachable, he will impart his wisdom and knowledge to us.
>
> My time of wandering awakened in me a hunger to learn. I was invited to attend a scripture study at a Baptist church,

which is where my love for God's word was born. Many years later, I would find myself back at the Catholic church, speaking at a retreat on the topic of scripture.

God is so gentle in the ways he guides us. After a journey of fifteen years, I returned to the Catholic church, enriched by my experiences. Transitions are never easy; actually they are usually rather arduous. My journey back was filled with questions, doubts, and lots of confusion as to where I belonged. A divinely inspired sequence of events, which included people God put in my path and books that landed in my lap, together with a gut-wrenching cry of surrender late one night, all culminated with a vision of where God wanted me to be. Exhausted and spent, a few weeks before Easter, I returned to the Catholic church. I am forever grateful for the time of wandering, where many a church opened their arms to me and brought me in. My spirituality has been deeply enriched by many, for which I am thankful.

Then, I "stumbled" upon The Alpha Course, a non-denominational evangelization program, in the spring of 2016, but there is no stumbling or happenstance with God, really. I was invited to a Catholic church, an hour away, to check out the program. After sitting through one session, I was sold and knew that somehow we had to incorporate this course curriculum into our church.

As our church team wrestled with how best to roll out this program, a neighboring Episcopal church, less than three miles away, was hosting the course, scheduled to start in a few weeks. God led us to our Episcopalian friends. To say we felt welcomed is an understatement. We were embraced with open arms and brought into their family. They coached and mentored our team, and a few months later they sent us on our way to run our first course. With proper training, one is made ready, as ready as one can be. And thankfully, the gap of unpreparedness is filled by the Holy Spirit's counsel. In our case, the counsel offered by the Holy Spirit came in the form of sweet neighbors at the Episcopal church. God wove friendship and unity as we shared in spreading the Good News in our community.

I recently attended a nationwide conference for this program, which gathered almost a thousand individuals, representing hundreds of different churches from multiple traditions. As we worshiped together, listened to presentations on building God's kingdom, and prayed as one, I became overwhelmed by the reality that we *are* one body, soaked in unity, if we so choose.

Forging the path for something new in church can be a struggle. I realized at this conference I am part of a larger group of believers, all laboring in the Lord's vineyard. I am not alone and I am part of the body of Christ. We all have much to learn from one another, if we are willing to explore a bit and collect some treasured souvenirs. Spending time learning about my Christian brethren has broadened my understanding of church. It has helped form how I love, pray, worship, and live; and it has taught me a thing or two about loving my neighbor.

Chapter 3

Early Expeditions

I enjoyed my sophomore year of college back home. The classes I took at the junior college and the rich fellowship with my church family helped prepare me to leave again the following fall. In many ways, I was more ready the second time around.

My first Sunday away at a state university, I attended Second Baptist Church. It would be my church home for the next three years. At the time, the congregation worshiped in their gymnasium, because the sanctuary was still being built. One of the first few weeks I was there, they introduced a new pastor, Dr. John Marshall. He asked that we call him by the name he most identified with, John 3:16. It was an exciting time to be at Second.

Every pastor has their preaching idiosyncrasies. Dr. Marshall would always tell us when we saw a *therefore* in scripture, we should ask ourselves what it's there for. Years later, the church would download his weekly sermons onto their website. I'd listen on long car rides from time to time. He adopted a new phrase in his later years that I just loved: "holiness matters most."

Dr. Marshall pastored this large church for more than twenty years. I have great admiration for pastors and congregations who find a way to stay together. Over the years, I've known a few pastors who

---

Some names in this chapter have been changed to protect the privacy of the individual.

served long-term pastoral roles at one church. I've met a few people who have attended one and only one church. They may visit others, but they call one church home. Further, the traditions of their church are so ingrained in them, they often don't know much about how other believers do church. I want to introduce you to one such friend of mine. She's always been Lutheran, and attended the white church with a tall steeple surrounded by fields in rural Indiana.

Meet Amy

We met through our husbands, who have been friends for years. It didn't take me long at all to home in on the fact that she's a Lutheran who loves her faith. What a treasure to befriend someone who can explain a faith tradition I knew little about.

> My church is more than 150 years old. It's a white building, and the steeple, with its gilded cross high in the air, can be seen from miles away. The church cemetery is across the road from the building. Inside, the church has wooden pews, and beautiful stained-glass windows that run nearly floor to ceiling of the two-story church. Each of the stained-glass windows has a round central piece that depicts various representations. One has fish and bread. One has a cross with INRI inscribed. Lots of woodwork. Up front, the white altar, with a depiction of the Lord's Supper carved into it, has not changed in all of my thirty-seven years. On top of the altar, the table holds a Bible, two candles, and on communion Sundays, the body and blood of Jesus. Above this is intricate artwork and architecture. The altar nearly fills the height of the two-story building as well. I've seen my church empty and I've seen it filled to capacity. I've seen her happy and I've seen her sad. I see the red candle that hangs in the sanctuary that is always lit to symbolize that God is always with us. I see my family, both the blood and church ones.
>
> I hear the rich beauty of our pipe organ, the congregation singing familiar hymns, the chatter of familiar friends after the

> service is over. As a mother now, I especially love that kids and babies are included in our services; including their cries, wails, and other noises. We have a huge bell up high in the bell tower. It is rung at the beginning of each service, and can be heard for miles around. It's always rung every All Saints' Day, once for each member of our church who has passed away in that year. Can you hear it?

Amy's church sounds remarkable. It is. I saw her get married there. It's not flashy or trendy, but points to long-standing tradition. When she wrote about her church, some of the words sounded familiar to me. She grew up two miles from this country church. When she was old enough, she'd ride her bike there. Her mom is the organist, so Amy would tag along with her when she went to practice at the church, and saw the church in a different way than one does on Sunday morning. With fondness, she recalled the pastors who served this church.

There are differences in her story too. Growing up Lutheran, she was baptized as an infant. She attended a parochial school. I'll let her tell you:

> I was baptized as an infant—I was just a couple weeks old. Around the baptismal font were my parents, the pastor, and my sponsors. Sponsors are those individuals chosen by the parents to help ensure the child is raised in the church in a Christ-centered way. My sponsors were an adult cousin and a couple who were close friends of my parents. At baptism, the child is given a candle that is lit from the Paschal candle. (Does everyone have a Paschal candle? The Paschal candle is a new candle each year, blessed during the Easter Vigil service. It stands next to the baptismal font each Sunday.) As the candle is handed over to the parents of the newly baptized, the pastor says "Receive this burning light . . . live always by the light of Christ . . ." These words were used at my baptism. I was able to hear these words at the baptisms of each of my daughters

and many other times throughout the years. I love the symbolism behind these words and this practice. Baptism at our church has the pastor use his hand to cup water out of the baptismal font and pour it over the head three times. He says "I baptize you in the name of the Father (water), the Son (water), and the Holy Spirit (water)." Obviously I don't remember my baptism, but I struggle to put into words the emotion involved in my daughters' baptisms. They wore the same outfit I wore for my baptism. They were wrapped in a blanket made by my grandmother who has been dead for more than ten years. My husband held them and I watched the pastor pour water over their tiny, innocent heads. And in that moment, it was like a force field went up protecting them. Nothing can happen to them now—they are God's. "God's own child I gladly say it, I am baptized into Christ; he because I could not pay it gave my full redemption price."

I went to a Lutheran school, so prayers, catechism, chapel, memory verses, and so forth were an important part of my daily school life. However, in seventh grade we began a confirmation class where this study intensified. We studied Martin Luther, church doctrine, liturgy, hymns, creeds, prayers, etc. This was a two-year study. Near the end of eighth grade, our class was confirmed—the whole class together. This included our school class as well as any public school kids that were the same age; because we did our study during the school day, any public school kids met with the pastor on Sunday afternoons to receive the same instruction. The confirmation process included a public examination in front of church during a church service, where our group (I think there were six in my class) stood before church and answered questions from the pastor. Some sample topics included the Ten Commandments and their meanings, the Apostles' Creed, the petitions of the Lord's Prayer, questions about the seasons of the church year, along with biblical references in support of each. Let me tell you—what a nerve-wracking time for a fourteen-year-old. The

> following Sunday, the confirmands went again to the front of the church for the rite of confirmation. We wore white robes and knelt at the altar. The pastor placed his hand on our head and blessed us. We also were assigned a confirmation verse; mine is Matthew 28:19–20. Our confirmation class was the first table to receive Holy Communion that day. While I think it was neat to receive communion for the first time with my confirmation class, I also wished I had been able to receive communion for the first time with my family. That's something I have questioned to this day.

Now in the fourth church I'd called home, I got involved with the college class at Second Baptist. It was a thriving group, including active adult volunteers. I didn't meet anyone at church outside of the college group for quite some time, but it was enough for me to settle into their family atmosphere. Each time I've set out to find a new church, usually because I find myself living in a new town, I look for a place where I belong. There are times I want to slip in and out of a Sunday morning service, depending on my mood. When I visit churches, I am largely looking for an encounter with Jesus rather than looking to meet a bunch of new people, but I do need my home church to feel like family.

Most Sunday mornings I think we all want to walk into a worship service and feel known. If we're introverted that can mean a quick wave, a hello, or a smile before we quickly find a seat. For extroverts, it can mean conversing with a group in the church lobby long after the majority of the crowd has left. Christ assures us that where two or three gather in his name, he is among us. In my church experience, that usually starts small and grows over time.

This college group was the Baptist church experience I knew, and then some. We had classes on Sunday morning, small groups during the week, visitation meetings on Monday nights, and multiple events and trips throughout the year. I learned a great deal about Bible study, started hearing names of theologians and writers like C.S. Lewis and Philip Yancey, and watched loving Christian families embody hospitality. These Christian brothers and sisters welcomed us into their homes when our families were hundreds of miles away. Second Baptist would also be my introduction to Bible studies by Beth Moore. She was brand new at the time, and a pioneer of video-recorded studies.

In my second year at Second, the building addition, which included the sanctuary, a front foyer, and several classrooms, reached completion. Just before they put down the carpet in the sanctuary, every member of the congregation was invited to sign our names on the floor, along with Bible verses that were important to us. I knew right where I would put my signature. I'd done business with God at so many altars by that point in my life, it wasn't even a question. I went right up to the space where the altar would be, took a few steps to the left of the pulpit location, and wrote my name in Sharpie marker. I wrote two verses beside my name:

> They look on the outward appearance, but the Lord looks on the heart.
>
> 1 Samuel 16:7

> The end of the matter; all has been heard. Fear God, and keep his commandments; for that is the whole duty of everyone.
>
> Ecclesiastes 12:13

In those days at Second, no one was around to tell me to wake up for church on Sundays (not that my mom ever had to), and I no longer attended a Christian university, where it would be frowned upon to skip church (even though I went because I wanted to), but I went every Sunday. Going to church had become an absolute habit for me. There's never been a time in my life I didn't go.

With the new addition, Second opened a church bookstore. This blew my mind, and for a long time I struggled with it. Jesus threw out the moneychangers in the temple. Surely he didn't want his church to be a business, did he? But of course, I realize now, church is a business of sorts. No way around it. This church sold these items at cost to its congregation. I've since been in a number of churches that do the same. It would seem it's the heart behind the business that makes it godly or not.

My paternal grandpa passed away in August of my senior year at college. He meant a lot to me, and although he could be a real handful, I mourned this loss deeply. Grandpa never went to church, and it occurred to me for the first time in a very real way that I might have a loved one spending eternity in hell. For months, I couldn't stand this thought, and wasn't able to figure out how to make peace with the unknowing. Several times, I found my way up front during the invitation call at my church. I knelt down at the altar in my spot, the one where I'd written Bible verses in Sharpie marker. There, I'd plead with God to save my grandpa, that somewhere along the way he had acknowledged Jesus as his savior. It would leave me weeping. After weeks of this emotional struggle, a mentor of mine, Ann, came and hugged me after the service. She told me it was okay to be sorry about my grandpa, but there came a time when we had to trust God with the lives of our loved ones. I thought of my relationship with Grandpa. He knew my mom, my siblings, and I were Christ-followers. I'd discussed what I believed with him. I handed the eternal outcome over to God.

The church I attend now doesn't have an invitation call at the end of our service. The pastor doesn't often lead us in the sinner's prayer, and there's not as great an emphasis on reaching lost souls for Jesus. At times, this bothers me. I think you have to find a balance. We should be bold about our faith and ask important questions about the state of a person's soul. Salvation is a private and personal thing though. I've also developed a certain level of trust in God to do that work. He is just and loving—the only one who truly knows the heart of human beings. The final judgment call isn't up to me. Since those days of my struggling with Grandpa's salvation and going through a similar process when I lost my dad, I've stopped trying to determine another person's relationship with God. Some things are beyond our complete understanding. It's where faith takes over.

I dated a Christian guy the summer before my senior year of college. A Nazarene. Another denomination I knew nothing about, but he was a godly man. We were at that age, early-to-mid-twenties, when we could stay up until the wee hours of the morning, and still function at work the next day. We spent hours discussing theology. One of the things we discussed often, likely because we weren't in agreement and were subtly trying to convince the other about the error of their ways, was whether believers could lose their salvation. We'd banter our points back and forth. I must have mentioned this area of dissension when I was talking with a lady in our church's children's ministry office. Immediately, she got a concerned look on her face. "Well, are you sure you should be dating him? I mean, what will you teach your children if you aren't in agreement?"

I don't recall what I said to her, but her question shocked me. I'd been to church with this guy. They absolutely preached God's word. Both of his parents were strong Christians, which was more than I could say about my own family. It never occurred to me there might be a theological point that would keep us apart. I had a lot of thinking to do.

A few days later, I stopped by our pastor's office, which I did on occasion during the workday. I was working at the church, and I had also become close with his daughter, so I got to know him on a more personal level. He always took the time to visit with me when I stopped by (and you guys, I was a nobody, really). His assistant told me to go on in because he wasn't working on his sermon for the week. That was the only time he had his door closed.

I asked him about the Nazarenes. We talked specifically about people holding to the belief that Christians can lose their salvation. While it was an enlightening discussion, he never told me what I needed to do in my relationship. He didn't tell me I'd have to find someone who agreed with me completely before I could date him. If I knew the man was a Christ-follower, I could comfortably pursue the relationship. I left feeling released somehow. Although I'd never been anything but Southern Baptist, I didn't have to date exclusively within my denomination. A few months later, the guy broke up with me and it was all for naught anyway. Still, I'd internalized the lesson. Christians didn't have to agree completely on every single theological point to do life together.

We'll probably debate things like this forever, or at least until Jesus comes again. I'm not telling you we have to stop noticing how our traditions vary from one another. I'm suggesting that rather than eagle-eye the differences, and demanding you're right, we learn from one another. We realize discovering new ways to worship Jesus can grow our faith. We accept faith must have a certain sense of mystery to it. It's exhausting to think you have it all figured out, and following a list of rules not only makes you legalistic, it damages relationships among friends and family.

Meet Quantrilla

I haven't met her in person, but she's such a cheerleader for her writer friends online. The day we meet in real life, I have the biggest hug reserved for her.

> I grew up in a conservative Seventh-Day Adventist (SDA) home. This meant there were things we didn't do or wear, food and drink items we didn't partake of, places we didn't go, that sort of thing. Conversely, there were things we always did: We attended church every Sabbath, a time of rest beginning sunset Friday and ending sunset Saturday, and I went to SDA schools. This in and of itself wasn't a bad thing, and I still consider myself a Christian whose membership is held at a local SDA church. The interesting part of this story is that I am a first-generation Seventh-Day Adventist. That means that I was born into the SDA church, compared to my parents who both came from other denominations into this tradition. My mother was raised Baptist, and my paternal grandmother raised her children in a similar fashion. According to my family, my mother always had a very decidedly spiritual bent, even in her formative years. She sang often and it was this very gift that brought her to a tent effort sponsored by one of the SDA churches in Gadsden, Alabama. She came to sing, but was deeply moved by the teaching presented each night, and the summer before she was to attend college, she was

baptized into the SDA church. This caused a huge rift between her and her family, especially her mother, and she found herself headed to Oakwood College (now Oakwood University), a small SDA liberal arts institution in Huntsville. My father's story was a bit different; it was his mother who became a Seventh-Day Adventist quite a few years after the majority of her children were grown and had their own children.

Because of many differing ways of denominational upbringing on both sides of my family, there were areas of friction, especially as it related to food, music, even style of worship. Family members who were used to their Saturdays looking a certain way were frustrated to say the least when changes were made to reflect new beliefs and convictions. In addition, once these convictions were espoused, some became rigid and inflexible. One such example was my graduation from graduate school. By this time, my mother had passed away, and many of her siblings had also become Seventh-Day Adventists and relocated to where my family lived in Florida. I was living in Atlanta at the time, and one of the promises I made to my mother was that I would continue my education after college. The graduation day was scheduled on a Saturday, and there was some back and forth conversation regarding the logistics of navigating the ceremony and getting the meal together afterward. One family member in particular decided that even after making the long-distance trip for the event, her family would not be attending the ceremony due to her convictions that it was a slight to the Sabbath to attend. She rallied my godmother, who was a large part of my support system, and convinced her to do the same. To add insult to injury, she stated that she was sure if my mother had been alive, she too would not have attended my graduation. This was a huge source of contention for me because my mother didn't share the same conviction on that particular issue, and I felt the family member used the memory of my mother to evoke a sense of guilt, rather than choosing to celebrate the accomplishment as a promise I had previously made to my mother.

Even as I began to reconsider the varied beliefs other Christians might have, I still thought I would be Southern Baptist my whole life. Honestly, I hadn't spent much time exploring the differences in what other traditions believed. I knew a family shouldn't baptize infants, because everyone should know the act of baptism doesn't save a person. I knew drinking was sinful, although I did order a fruity, frozen *alcoholic* drink on my twenty-first birthday. Many things I thought I knew. In addition, I still looked at some churches with a great deal of skepticism. In my college town, there is a large charismatic style church. I still didn't know what to do with what I grew up knowing as "the holy rollers." They spoke in tongues, raised their hands during worship songs, and rolled in the aisles (thus the name). Other than one Christian concert, I'd never stepped foot in a church like this. A friend of mine from Second dated a boy from this church for a while, and as her friends, a group of us were concerned. Only years later would I settle on the fact there are wonderful Christian brothers and sisters in the pentecostal tradition too. They saved my brother from a lifestyle that would have likely destroyed him. I had to repent of the judgment I had passed on those who worship in the Spirit in ways I did not understand.

Two years later, the university handed me a diploma. I had not a clue what to do with it, and I didn't have a single contact in my general field of study, which was communication. After working part-time at Second Baptist in their weekday preschool program, considering law school options (more schooling might keep me from having to find a job), and filling out dozens of job applications, a public relations company in St. Louis offered me an internship. I took the job and started asking my friends and mentors questions about where to live and where to worship. I was about to encounter church life as a single career woman, and I was excited to begin.

The pastors at the various churches I attended in St. Louis were distant leaders to me. I didn't know any of them personally. At one point, I was struggling in a dating relationship. Actually, you probably wouldn't even call it that. I had fallen for a guy I had no business falling for. I can blame some of it on naivety, and some on being far away from family who might have offered more accountability. But mostly I blame myself. Anyway, I was so distraught over this relationship one day, I needed to reach out to someone who would give me advice I could trust. Although I loved my dad, he was unable to offer this kind of wisdom. I realized in my past, various pastors had played this role in my life. So I emailed Dr. Marshall. I hadn't seen him in three or four years by that point but I gave him an update, telling him I'd fallen for a guy who was obviously trouble. His response came quickly, short and direct. "Traci, you must protect your heart at all cost. If you have to change careers, move to a new city, whatever it takes. Leave this man behind." He confirmed what the Spirit had been telling me in my soul all along, but it helped to receive the advice from someone I respected.

In a matter of months, God worked out a whole new career path for me. I left that bad situation behind, and in time (also through a handful of Christian therapy sessions), my heart did heal. The whole situation showed me the importance of not just finding a church to worship in, but a community to walk through life with in every way. We need the accountability of God's people. It's easy to attend church faithfully every Sunday, and do stinking living the other six days. I know—I've done it.

I was a young adult in my twenties, starting out in my career, when Mom delivered some devastating news from home. After twenty-some years of marriage, three kids and a handful of grandkids, my parents were getting a divorce. For years, Mom shared her life with a man who didn't share her faith. Although they had a home life together, their social lives didn't match up. Mom enjoyed being active in her church and visiting with neighbors and family. Dad spent much of his time with drinking buddies. After their kids left the house, his drinking got worse. She started hearing rumors of excessive drinking, possible drug use and promiscuity. They tried a few counseling sessions with Mom's pastor but the marriage was over. As a godly woman she never planned on things ending this way. From 250 miles away my parents' divorce hit me hard. We were Baptist. We didn't believe in divorce. Life is more complicated than that though.

What a blessing it was knowing Mom's church supported her during this time. She didn't walk that hard road alone. They loved her and over the years, in her new church as well, continued asking her to serve in a variety of roles. Mom is my biggest mentor in the faith, an amazing woman who is willing to share her experiences with anyone who could benefit from it. The primary story you'll hear will be about the mercy, grace, and redemption Christ offers us all.

During my years in St. Louis I visited a few churches in other traditions. No one noticed if I missed a Sunday or two where I was attending at that point. It occurred to me I enjoyed observing how others worshiped. These Christians were my brothers and sisters too, and this fact settled ever more deeply within me. As I began branching out to other traditions, I had no difficulty settling into any evangelical pew. Baptist, Presbyterian, Methodist: we had a lot of similarities.

I also remember visiting St. Alphonsus Liguori "Rock" Catholic Church (when you live in a city named after a saint, it seemed like the thing to do) one Sunday. I snuck into a seat in the middle of the sanctuary, in the middle of a row, hoping to go entirely undetected. I went alone. When experiencing a brand new worship service, I still like to go alone. If something goes wrong, the only person subjected to the embarrassment is me. The group gathered there that morning was by far the most diverse I'd ever sat among at church. About five minutes after the service was scheduled to start, an African American priest started making his way up the center aisle. You heard him before you saw him. You smelled him before you saw him too. Wait, that came out wrong. I know now, he was swaying a thurible of burning incense back and forth, calling out "Praise Gods" and "Hallelujahs" as he slowly made his way down the middle row. Many in the crowd responded to his call to worship. The service had gone on for about ninety minutes when they began preparations for communion, which I knew I couldn't participate in (I didn't recognize much of that particular Mass compared to the few I'd attended as a teenager, but I remembered that part), so as the parishioners started making their way forward to receive the body and blood of Jesus, I made my exit.

I had other notable run-ins with Catholicism during my years in St. Louis. I toured the Cathedral Basilica. I was so moved by being in the cathedral. I wondered at all the candle displays, having no idea what they were for but appreciating how they helped the ambiance of the vast sanctuary. After my tour, I bought my own rosary, because again it seemed like the right thing to do. I knew my Catholic friends were true Christ-followers and the cross I saw on that necklace was a symbol of our Christian faith. Maybe it was here, for the first time, I began wanting a deeper connection with my Catholic brothers and sisters. I wasn't sure what I would ever do with the rosary, but I remembered the effect it had on my high school friend and her family when they lost their mother. My mom and I had attended the visitation, where they had prayed the rosary, and it seemed to bring them great comfort, holding the beads in their hand as they recited the prayers. How did that one prayer go? "Hail Mary, full of grace, the Lord is with thee. . . ." Would I ever recall any more of it than that?

Another time, I was heading out of town via train on a business trip. I met a coworker at the station early on a Wednesday morning. Our client was traveling with us, and he got there shortly after we did. We walked over to greet him, and I tried hard not to stare. He had ash smeared on his forehead, in the shape of a cross. I racked my brain, trying to think of what could have caused this. Maybe he tended to the fireplace right before leaving his house that day ? Some soot on his overcoat from a bonfire he'd been to? A car fire? How did it happen to be in the shape of a cross? Once we were seated on the train, I asked my coworker about it. For the first time, in my mid-twenties, I learned about Ash Wednesday, the first day of the Lenten season in the Western Christian calendar.

Even as I visited these new churches, I didn't give any thought to leaving the only denomination I'd ever known. As I considered where I might attend if I left my current church, it never occurred to me I would stop being "Baptist." Years later, when I stumbled across Micha Boyett's words in her book, *Found,* I nodded my head in agreement, because I got her. "I figured I'd find a Bible church or a nondenominational church. But never had I thought I'd actually leave. Being Baptist was so tattooed in my way of experiencing scripture and worship and community. . . ."

Understand, I'm not going to tell you what tradition God would have you leave or join. For some of us, family ties and faith ties are one and the same strand. In some ways, I'll always consider myself a Baptist. The connection runs deep. I knew it was acceptable to explore though. My extended family had come from varying denominational backgrounds. Those in the church-at-large who loved me would love me regardless of what tradition I chose. If you end up leaving behind the tradition of your childhood, as I have, you will take parts of them with you. I hope you find love and acceptance along the way as well.

A close friend of mine began attending an Evangelical Presbyterian Church (EPC), which was located closer to where I worked and lived than the church I was attending at the time. They had a large, active singles group, and I visited a few times. This church was my first experience with an older church building. On Sundays, I would drive into an affluent part of St. Louis, often parking in the neighborhood behind the church because parking at the church itself was limited. I'd walk into the church with other families who were dressed in their Sunday best (although really, their everyday clothes were probably nicer than anything I donned when I attended church). They actually came to church from the distinguished older homes, while I just parked my car on their streets.

Inside the stone building, the sanctuary even smelled old. The wooden pews were aged, with faded red cushions added years prior for comfort. I'd been inside several Catholic cathedrals, and this church rivaled them in its beauty and charm.

This Presbyterian church was my first experience outside of my Southern Baptist bubble. I never joined the church, because they didn't do an altar call and I didn't have any idea how to join a church if I didn't walk down the aisle during the invitation hymn and let the pastor know I wanted to move my letter of membership. That's how the Baptists did it, and it was all I knew.

I couldn't have even told you how Presbyterians and Southern Baptists differ (today I could—sort of). I'd found a singles group that was a good fit and that's why I stayed. Right away, I noticed a couple of differences. We set out to do a group Bible study, I don't remember the topic, and the singles minister suggested a commentary to buy for our personal study time. These Presbyterians took their study of God's word seriously. Also, it was not at all uncommon for people to meet up for a beer and discuss theology. Wine was served at showers and other special events. There wasn't a major emphasis on the consumption of alcohol (like I'd accused the Catholics of in my younger days), but it was prevalent in the lives of the evangelical Presbyterians I got to know.

Most Sundays, we'd hear sermons from Pastor Adam. Several professors from a nearby seminary attended this church, even taking the pulpit as guest speakers from time to time. I learned a great deal from Adam. Although I never met him directly, I admired his preaching style. He seemed well liked by many.

It had been years since I'd been part of a church that had pastoring issues. I'd forgotten the pain and confusion that comes when a pastor suddenly resigns from a church. When I heard, through the church rumor mill, that Pastor Adam was under a great deal of scrutiny, I got a somewhat familiar feeling in my gut. They were after their pastor! As it turned out, Pastor Adam had preached a particular sermon a few weeks prior to the now-ensuing investigation. A fine message, but one he did not write in its entirety. The man had succumbed to some unknown pressure and plagiarized a large portion of this sermon. This is never an acceptable thing, but when members of your congregation make a living studying fine theologians and the sermons they offer the world, it's a huge mistake. It only took a short amount of time for the church powers-that-be to decide; Pastor Adam would be asked to resign.

I had such a loose affiliation with this church as a whole, I wasn't privy to any meetings where his future was discussed. Although I have wondered since then, I don't know if any grace was extended to Adam by the elders or other church leadership. What sort of pressure is a man under to feel the need to plagiarize a sermon? I thought back to the pastors of my childhood church, Mt. Pleasant.

Had they known months before the scandal started that their relationship was changing with certain members of the church? Were there harsh words spoken? Cold shoulders turned? How does one continue to "perform" under such circumstances? The church notoriously struggles with knowing what to do with its own when they fall from grace. I'm not passing judgment on those who made the decisions. The occurrence just brought up a bunch of questions in my mind. Questions I still wrestle with today.

Talk with anyone who's been in church for a number of years, and they'll share their stories about church discipline, fallen pastors, and church splits. Or maybe they won't talk to you about those times. They are some of the rawest moments a person experiences in the church. Often times, it seems we don't want to talk about it. But maybe we'd all be better off if we did.

Meet Sarah

I met Sarah through some writing groups I'm a part of on Facebook. I'd known her a few years before I made the connection she lives close to my mom in the south. It's a small world after all.

> After my husband and I married, we thought we'd found our church. We adored our pastor and his wife, and we could see ourselves raising our children in this church body. A few months into our marriage, I began working in the church office. Life was moving along for us. We began hosting a weekly small group in our home and felt like we'd found our forever church home.
>
> The day Joe, our elder chairman, arrived at our home and told us they were placing our pastor under church discipline was, well . . . difficult. To say we were shocked would be an understatement. At the time we had no idea it would affect us so deeply. We were in our late twenties and had never dealt with this level of conflict. I thought things like this only happened when a pastor was unfaithful to his wife or stole money from the church. My husband and I struggled to

understand the charges being leveled against a man we cared about so much.

We watched the church body divide over whether our pastor should be dismissed. The elder had a way of explaining things that made you think you understood, but still left a few questions. I think that sense of doubt we felt was God telling us something wasn't right.

In a heartbreaking moment, the church body voted to dismiss our beloved pastor. His wife asked me to pick a side and in my confusion, I questioned their loyalty. I was unsure of what to believe and just wished I could fix everything. The tears I cried over those months left me raw and uncertain. We lost our church friends, some left and some just turned their backs on us, feeling we were on the "other" side of whatever they believed. They never asked us, they just assumed they knew how we felt.

I was still the church secretary, so life went on and the elder chairman took over as interim pastor. Months later, everyone was settling into this "new" church body, after so many families chose to leave. My husband and several other men were appointed as deacons, then they formed the pastor search committee. As a deacon, my husband was responsible for the computers, server, and other miscellaneous resources in the church office. One night he stayed up all night working in his home office. The next morning, he asked me who was in the pastor's office the day before. It was only Joe, the interim pastor, and myself.

He showed me website addresses and the time stamped on them could only point to Joe. He was hiding a pornography addiction. My husband went to another elder and together they confronted Joe. When he denied it, the matter went before the church body. Suddenly all those allegations against our old pastor were looking quite different, as Joe became a completely different person. We could see malice and evil intent as he fought to keep control of the church. It was a difficult six months for us. Many people didn't believe what the facts clearly showed.

> Even after the elder was forced out of the church under church discipline, his heart remained unrepentant.
>
> We brought in a new pastor from another state and our church slowly began to heal, though not without paying a steep price. After another year, we decided it was time to change churches. We were still hurting over the abandonment of so many friends. It felt like the sins of others were the rule by which we were judged. My husband and I were leery of getting involved with a church for the next nine years. We watched each pastor and elder carefully, looking for signs of a possible issue. I think it would be easy to blame the church body for the hurt, but it was a difficult time for everyone. After fifteen years we still do not have contact with those original church friends. Do we have regrets? Absolutely. But, looking back I don't know that we could have handled it any differently.

At my church in St. Louis, a search committee was formed, we heard from a few guest speakers, and the church hired a new minister within months. He was an intellectual, with a formal manner of speaking, and I had a hard time connecting. Around the same time, the singles' minister took a new job out of town and the dynamics of that group began to change. I was attending a women's Bible study at the time but it wasn't enough for me to feel completely connected. Before long, I began looking for another church.

My first inclination was always to head back to my people, the Southern Baptists. My friend started attending an Evangelical Free church and I visited a few times, but it never felt like the right place for me. I found a flourishing Baptist church in south St. Louis. I liked the pastor and the church was growing so rapidly, they were in the midst of building an entirely new campus. For the first time, I went to a church that had a coffee bar.

Although I was unaware of it at the time, I would only live in St. Louis for a few more months anyway. I met a man, not at church as I'd always thought I would, but at a karaoke establishment (okay, a bar), through mutual friends. He swept me right off my feet and right out of town. For the first time in my life, I wouldn't call the state of Missouri my home. We made plans to move to Michigan, his home state, where the Great Lakes really are that beautiful, and we do get that much snow.

One Sunday, a short time before we married and moved away, we planned on attending worship at my new church. We'd had bad weather the night before, the mix of snow and ice Missouri can get, and they'd canceled church that morning. We didn't realize that and drove there anyway. While sitting in the parking lot for a few minutes, trying to figure out if they were having church or not, the pastor pulled up in his car. He'd come down to the church in case there were people, like us, who hadn't heard about the closing. My fiancé rolled down the driver's side window, got the news about the closing, and asked the pastor if he wanted to sit in the SUV for a few minutes. We were the only ones in the parking lot, so he got in to chat. We told him about our upcoming move, and he suggested we go to the website for a big church in Chicago called Willow Creek. In recent years this church has undergone intense scrutiny in the media following sexual harassment allegations against its senior pastor. At this time, the church was thought of as an evangelical example to follow. Willow Creek had compiled a list of churches across the country who had joined its association. The churches on this list usually, at the very least, offered a thriving environment. When we moved to Michigan, we used Willow Creek's listings to find a few churches to visit. The first thing I checked for was a Southern Baptist church in our new town, but there weren't many Southern Baptists that far North. I didn't find a church in my denomination-of-origin close to us. For the second time in my life, I found myself considering a potential church home outside of the faith tradition of my childhood.

Chapter 4

Family of God

A few weeks before I got married, I went to stay with my family and finalize wedding plans. We'd decided to have an outdoor wedding at my dad's place (at the time Mom was still in the house where I grew up and Dad had put a trailer on the back of the property). I didn't have any qualms about marrying Ryan. My nerves came from wondering how my mom and dad would get through the day. What do family photos look like when the parents are newly divorced? For years I had prayed my dad would show up to walk me down the aisle. Mom and I had discussed backup plans in case he was a no-show. Now, the divorce added even more layers of complexity. The wedding went swimmingly though (April showers in Missouri and all). The morning of our wedding, a crack of thunder rang out loud and clear about six in the morning. I heard Mom tiptoeing down the hall at the same time, and from the sleeping pallet I'd made on the couch (we had several out of town guests so I'd given up my childhood bedroom) I said, "Mom, isn't it a great day for an indoor wedding?" We called our neighbors, who were caretakers for the Mt. Olive Church of my childhood, and they graciously told us we could have our wedding there. We moved the few decorations we had to the church, gathered up the stored items that had accumulated in the choir loft and had a country wedding—inside. Pastor Chuck married us that day. In so many ways, it felt like the faith of my childhood, with all of its church experiences, was coming full circle.

As newlyweds, Ryan and I settled on the "other side of the state." That's what folks on the Lake Michigan side call the Detroit area (and vice versa). It was important to both of us that our marriage get started on the right spiritual foot. During our engagement, we'd gone to a weekend retreat called "Engagement Encounter." The conference took place at Camp Geneva (a Reformed Church conference center), on Lake Michigan's shoreline. Over the course of two days, presentations were made on multiple topics for engaged couples to discuss before getting married. There was a panel composed of three married couples: newlyweds, a mid-life couple, and seasoned veterans. It was helpful to have the topics presented to us, and we covered things we'd never thought to talk about together. I only remember a few other couples from that weekend, because mostly I only had eyes for my fiancé at that point. My roommate and my fiancé's roommate in the dorms were also engaged. They'd met on eHarmony. I found this so interesting at the time, although since then, I've known several other couples who met their mate online and lived happily ever after.

The other couple I remember broke my heart, because their own hearts were absolutely broken that weekend. I'm sure they went on this retreat anticipating a loving, fun-filled time away with one another. But some topic, or two, caused them difficulty. It was painful to watch them go through the sessions, crying guttural tears as they dealt with their private issues. I've thought of them often over the years, hoping they found God's best for them, whatever that looked like.

Ryan and I didn't grow up with the same faith experiences. As a child, he attended a Church of God church about forty-five minutes away from home. They joined his grandparents at the church where his dad had grown up. This gave him a special relationship with his grandparents, and, as a result, he places a high value on family. However, it was a small church. Ryan didn't attend church with people he knew from school or even from his small town. He never participated in a youth group.

Oh goodness how God must have chuckled when he brought Ryan and me together. We are both Christ-followers, but we don't, and won't, have identical faith walks. I always had this image of the guy I would marry. He would read his Bible (possibly in the original languages) all the time and we'd have endless discussions about theology. Ryan and I have had a number of conversations over the years about our faith, including specifics about our individual beliefs and what faith experiences we hoped to create in our home. However, reading the Bible together happens sporadically, and while I share thoughts with him when I'm doing my daily Bible reading and he sends me verses from Proverbs warning against living with a nagging wife, the deep theological discussions aren't quite what I envisioned.

I'm unashamedly one of those people who hates to miss a single Sunday at church (admittedly, there's also an ounce or two of guilt that exists when I don't go), so one of the first things I did upon settling in to our new neighborhood was reference that Willow Creek church directory and make a plan. I already knew there were no Southern Baptist churches in the area, which put me at square one. Ryan grew up in church but hadn't gone with any regularity since high school. In spite of the fact that I'd always been a total church girl who memorized Bible verses for fun and never had a time in my life when I didn't attend church, God paired me with a man who didn't express quite as much passion about Bible study or church life. His faith is a more practical one. I'm thankful for his godly wisdom and willingness to attend church with our family, something my mom never got to experience with her husband.

The first church we visited was a Baptist church. (I know, I know. What is it in us that clings to the comfortable?) I'm not sure what Baptist affiliation this church was, but it wasn't Southern Baptist (remember, I'd checked). We parked our car in the parking lot, Ryan looked around at the crowd walking in, and said, "This isn't our church." I've learned over the years that he can choose the right church for him based on what he observes in the parking lot. What he meant in this case was the attire of the people attending the service. The women wore dresses and the men were in shirts and ties. This isn't my husband's style, not even during the work week. At church, he associates this with boring music, an insistence on a lot of rules, and a pastor he at best wouldn't relate to, and at worst, would put him to sleep. He was right, the service was a bit on the traditional, old-school side. Not a church we felt comfortable attending together. We only visited the one time.

The following Sunday, we tried out Christ the King Church. We visited Christ the King one time and knew we'd found our first church home as a married couple. Ryan felt fine with the people in the parking lot that Sunday (mostly jeans, shorts, and t-shirts). A few months later, when the church recruited some authority-hungry (read grumpy) men to serve as parking lot attendants, he felt less fine about those in the parking lot who tried to tell him he couldn't park his car at the end of a row so as to avoid door dings. We were pretty locked into the church by that point, so he dealt with it.

Christ the King was a nondenominational church. They were new to the grounds where they worshiped, which had been an inner-city camp for years. When the church that owned the campground decided to sell it off, they wanted to sell it to a religious organization. That's how Christ the King came to have gorgeous lakefront property. There were a few local building contractors who wouldn't have stepped one foot in that church as a result. We met in the gymnasium, and there were long-term plans to build an addition that included a sanctuary. The chairs would always be set up for Sunday mornings, but then cleared for drama practice, or for vacation Bible school activities, or to host dinners. It took me back to my early days at Second Baptist, when we met in their gymnasium. We haven't been back to Christ the King since moving to the "Lake Michigan side of the state," but I'd like to someday.

Pastor Bob was the heart of this church. Much like the prodigal son, pastor Bob had some years of wild living before being radically saved as a young adult. Ryan still recalls a story Pastor Bob told us one Sunday of stealing a guitar from someone's house. As a new Christian, he felt strongly convicted about owning a stolen guitar, but he had entered the house from the back and had no recollection of the exact residence from where he'd taken it. Being rescued from such a hard past meant the words he shared from the pulpit came from a different place. He knew firsthand the difference Christ makes in a life, and this knowledge made him passionate. Every word he shared with us came from a hard-earned wisdom without an ounce of judgment. It was a great fit for our first church.

As I mentioned, Christ the King is nondenominational. I couldn't have told you much about what that meant. I knew nothing about acronyms like TULIP (the five points of Calvinism: total depravity, unconditional election, limited atonement, irresistible grace, and perseverance of the saints). I probably could have told you Martin Luther was a Catholic-turned-Lutheran, but I didn't know one other thing about the Reformation. I'd never heard of Christian traditions such as Eastern Orthodox or Plymouth Brethren. John Wesley and John Calvin were the names of good Christian men who had been church leaders a long time ago. Right? From my experience, I'm among the majority, especially in evangelical circles. Many Christians seem to think they have enough on their hands trying to study the Bible, without knowing about things like church history, or finer points of doctrine and traditions that seem worlds apart from our own daily lives. What I did know was Christ the King Church had a sweet spirit. The pastor preached from God's Word every Sunday. They prayed as a congregation, and had a heart for evangelism. Lives were made more Christ-like through their ministry. God seemed to smile upon this church.

How do people decide on a church home? For some, the church of their childhood is the only church they'll ever know. More and more of us, though, move on from the faith of our early days and try a new tradition. The reasons why are as diverse as the church stories each of us are living. The more I examine the ways we worship Jesus, the more I'm convinced God is big enough to embrace our differences. I was at another nondenominational church once and saw a young mom take her little girl up to the communion table. Carrying her on her hip, she reached down and took a piece of the bread, dipped it in the juice, and gave her daughter the body and blood of

Jesus Christ. Then she took some for herself. At a Catholic church for an Ash Wednesday service, a young girl, about eight years old, recited the learned responses well (much better than I did), and out of the corner of my eye, I watched her mom place her own hands over her daughter's, positioning them together in a posture of praying, just so, before going forward to receive the ashes. We have a young man with special needs at our church, and he took communion for the first time as a teenager. His mom worried maybe he wasn't able to comprehend the full meaning behind the elements before receiving them. After meeting with the pastor, the parents let their son join them at the table. The matter had been decided. At the end of each Sunday morning, we're all just trying to find a church home in every sense of the word, you know?

Meet Pauline

When I meet someone from a new faith tradition, I become slightly overzealous. I could pepper them with question after question. The friends I've made are so gracious to answer anything I ask. They even claim to learn a few things from me as well. I guess we're on the right track. I met Pauline on Facebook, and while we have not met in person, I consider her a close sister in Christ. Here's part of her story:

> There is a story told of the Roman Catholic saint, Therese of Lisieux, in which, as a child, she pondered how it might be that all the souls in heaven might not be equally happy. It troubled her sweet soul deeply. Another family member (her mother? sister? I can't remember) had her fetch a tumbler and thimble and fill them both with water. Then she asked which one was fuller. Therese answered that they were both so full no water could be added to either, but clearly one had a greater capacity. Through this, the young Therese understood all the souls in heaven are completely filled with the love and joy of God—but our cooperation with God's grace in us during our lives expands our capacity to be so filled with his joy in the age to come.

I knew and loved this story deeply during my childhood, growing up in a devoutly Roman Catholic family. My mother is Roman Catholic, raised in the traditions developed before Vatican II, and my father supported her raising us Catholic, though he does not affiliate with any particular faith tradition.

I was nurtured on the stories of heroes from the Bible and the history of the church, from its earliest days of persecution through to the twentieth century. During high school, I considered being a nun, thinking a life of prayer the obvious response to God's love. I looked at a few religious orders, and while they were beautiful, I never had an "a-ha" moment of thinking I'd found the right one where God had called me, so I didn't pursue it further.

Being raised in a family of faith from my earliest days, I don't remember a time I didn't know God loved me, he had sent his son to save me (John 3:16), we are saved by God's freely given grace (Eph. 2:8-9), and the appropriate response to such a gift of love is to work out our salvation with fear and trembling (Phil. 2:12).

The few times as a young adult I explored other traditions, both Christian and non-Christian, sooner or later, I missed the sacraments, the tangible experiences of God's deep love for his people. Over and over, like the prodigal son in the gospel, I was drawn back.

As an adult, I was married in the church to a wonderful man who was raised in a Catholic family but had been baptized Episcopalian. He converted to Catholicism after a profound experience in one of the historical churches in Cappadocia while there serving on an Air Force tour of duty. Our primary officiant at the wedding was a newly consecrated bishop whom I'd known since he was an associate pastor and I was a child. Once we were settled in our parish as newlyweds, I served as a lector (lay reader of scripture at Mass) and a catechist for adults becoming Catholic.

I was deeply fulfilled, living a life of faith within the spiritual practices of the Roman Catholic church, and it was within this context that one day, when I was discussing church history with an Orthodox priest through our mutual involvement in a chaplaincy program, both lay and ordained, for the local sheriff's office, I made the offhand remark that I knew the differences between our two churches.

And I can still hear his words, "Do you?"

I gave him the short form of the Schism of 1054, which I had learned in fifth grade religion class, and he encouraged me to go read about the belief and practice of the early church. I knew both the Orthodox Christian church and the Roman Catholic church made a claim to be the Church on earth, established by Christ. I was sure it was "my side" who was right. In my pride, I thought I'd confirm what I had been taught and convince him of the truth of Roman Catholicism's claim to be the One True Church. (May God have mercy on me for my extreme pride and lack of charity!)

So I began reading, first about how the Great Schism had happened, and then about the belief and practice of the early church as a whole. As I read, I found myself going back to the Bible, and in the context of knowing the belief and practice of the early church, the Bible had a deeper harmony as a whole than I had ever experienced while reading it before. It wasn't just that it made sense intellectually, but it resonated holistically within my soul in a whole new way. The tremendous gift of salvation and the depth of the love of God leapt out at me from the pages of scripture in new ways like never before.

Each thing I learned showed me Orthodox Christianity had the tools to help me know and be filled with Christ himself more completely. It was like my soul was being stretched, being given a tiny bit more capacity to be filled with God's love, but it was only a glimpse of how much more was possible through this ancient yet new-to-me way to live the Christian life.

I went to my first Divine Liturgy in an Orthodox church, and the experience of this form of worship drew me in completely. The richness of the prayers, which have been prayed by Christians since the earliest years of Christianity, made the cloud of witnesses from Hebrews 12:1 even more present and real than ever before, not just a theological abstraction. That happened with a lot of the Bible, actually. Passages that had seemed beautiful and largely poetic had plain meanings within the context of the lived experience of the Orthodox church handed down through the ages. My understanding of theological concepts began to grow and change.

I experienced the reality that the Christian life and traditional disciplines of liturgical worship, prayer, fasting, and almsgiving were incredibly effective tools for deepening one's capacity to be filled with the light and life of Christ himself. While Catholicism certainly has retained these elements, they grew in meaning as I spent more time among my Eastern Christian brothers and sisters. It was a difference that yielded a deeper humility and seriousness about the Christian life than I was accustomed to, and it was extraordinarily attractive.

After a time on this journey, I realized my beliefs were no longer in communion with the Roman Catholic church. I felt the tug of God in my heart calling me to become part of the Orthodox Christian church. At this time I stopped attending Mass and participating in the sacramental life of the Catholic church. It was three years before my children and I were received into the Orthodox church, mostly out of an inordinate amount of caution to ensure it wouldn't overly stress my marriage. My husband had not accompanied me on my theological and historical quest. My children and I went this way alone, though with his blessing.

This time felt like a sacramental wasteland, going through the years without either the opportunity for sacramental confession or communion. I even had a dream in which I was somehow attending a Mass offered by then Pope Benedict XVI, and he offered me Holy Communion. I shook my head, indicating that I couldn't receive, and he compassionately offered to hear my confession. I had to communicate to him that I was

> following where Christ was leading me, and I couldn't confess that as sin. And in the dream, after I explained this, His Holiness walked sadly away.
>
> As I write, we are nearly entering Lent; this year at Pascha (Easter) will be the fifth since our family's reception into the Orthodox church. The treasures within the way of life known as Orthodox Christianity, as imperfectly as I receive and practice them, and the very real experience of having tools to help me draw nearer to our Lord Jesus Christ continue to leave me surprised by joy and by the expansiveness of his love and mercy.
>
> May He be glorified by this and all things!

Eventually, I became more involved at Christ the King. There was a lady who loved theater, and she directed a lot of plays and skits at the church. I acted in a few of those, which I enjoyed. I taught children's Sunday school for a while. Toward the end of our time there, the children's director asked me if I would lead the children's worship on Sunday mornings. They prerecorded the music for Sunday mornings, with singing and actions. My job would be to stand up front, alone, and be the live person singing and doing the actions while the video ran in the background. When he asked me, I thought back to my days at Mt. Pleasant. One of the main lessons I took to heart in those days was serving the church however it was needed. I had a pretty good grasp of my gifts by that point, and they didn't include leading children's worship with movement. But there was a need, and I could fill it. So I did.

I've always thought Ryan would get more involved in church when the right opportunities for him came along. Christ the King didn't have a men's group necessarily, but they hosted an annual wildlife dinner with a guest speaker, and served things like pheasant pasta and squirrel stew. He enjoyed that event. For a while, he attended a men's group that met in a guy's barn. In addition, he is always encouraging when I ask him about a ministry I feel led to participate in myself.

It was at Christ the King that Ryan and I attended our first small group together. We're quite a combination; the lifelong Bible student sitting on the edge of her seat and her husband, who attends a lot of corporate meetings, keeping an eye on the clock to make sure we end on time. A group of about eight of us came together to discuss a popular evangelical study at the time, Rick Warren's *The Purpose-Driven Life: What On Earth Am I Here For?* Overall, it was a good experience. I remember the study being evangelism-driven; how to share your faith in practical ways with people in your community. The first line of the study has never left me, "It's not about you." What an excellent outlook on faith. Ultimately, no matter what tradition you call home, it's about Christ.

We'd been married three years when tragedy struck my family back home. My husband took a late night call from my brother, telling us Dad was being taken by ambulance to the local hospital. Things didn't look good. Approximately thirty minutes later, we received a second call. Dad was gone. Immediately, we threw some things in a bag and headed to Ryan's parents. It was late at night, and we planned on staying overnight there because it was a bit closer. We'd drive the remaining nine hours in the morning, when we were fresh. Upon arriving at their house, I realized in the hurried packing I had done, I'd left my Bible at home. This seemingly little thing devastated me. Through tears, I asked my father-in-law if I could borrow his Bible. I turned to the Psalms (those of you who have walked with God for any length of time understand why) and I poured out my grief. I was overwhelmed by the sadness of losing my dad. No matter what your religious convictions are, family is family. Grieving over the loss of my dad has changed with time, but will never go away completely.

We were in Missouri for about a week, making funeral arrangements, meeting about Dad's estate. Since my parents were divorced when Dad died, the responsibility of the estate fell on my two brothers and me. By this point in my life, I had friends all over the country. Brothers and sisters in Christ from many of the churches I had called home. In the throes of grief, though, I didn't call on a single one of them. The people who surrounded us as we mourned our dad and laid him to rest there at Mt. Olive Church cemetery were the loved ones of my childhood. I'm sure those of you who grew up in a small town, but no longer live there, can relate. If you didn't grow up in one place long enough to feel like you have a hometown, let me try to explain. I'm in my forties, and when I go back to my hometown, I still say I'm going home. I have never returned to Mt. Pleasant, but I frequently worship with those at First Baptist when I return home for a visit. These days, I don't know the pastor, music director, or many faces in the congregation, but it still feels like I've gone home to church.

When we laid my dad to rest, First Baptist provided our family and loved ones with a meal after the funeral. The funeral home where we held the service was full of people I'd known my whole life. I leaned on them to give me the strength to say goodbye. My church at the time, Christ the King, felt a million miles away. It seemed like my made-up life, and my real one was right there in small town Missouri. No one at my Michigan church knew about Dad's passing, so they offered no condolences. I don't fault them at all. It was my choice to not call and let them know about my loss. They were a part of a new life that didn't mesh with my old one in any way. I had all the support I needed from loved ones in my past.

When I returned to Michigan, my employers were kind to me. I took some more time off. My neighbors and friends from work sent sympathy cards. I realized we'd started to build a community of sorts, but it felt distant from where I'd come from. I wondered if I'd ever feel like any place in Michigan would truly feel like home.

Chapter 5

Home Church

Within a year of burying my dad, we moved closer to my husband's side of the family. This was in part due to the fact that the auto industry was experiencing financial troubles (again). Friends of ours started to worry about the security of their jobs, and many found work elsewhere. My husband started looking too and found a job on the west side of the state. We had also decided once we were settled in, we'd start thinking about having a child. We figured it would take a few weeks to sell our house, hopefully making a small profit, then we'd find a new home and start a family of our own. Best laid plans don't always match up with what God has in store for us though. Had we known it would take us two and a half years to sell our house, right in the midst of automotive layoffs, during the housing market crash of 2007, would we have made the same choices? It's hard to say, but God's goodness took us through a most challenging time. We entered a chapter of our life together where we'd have to rely on one another, and our community, in ways we never had before.

I, of course, started church shopping right away. At first we attended the church Ryan's parents had been attending, a Church of God congregation, the denomination Ryan had known as a child.

The long-time pastor at this church had recently resigned, moving away from the area. My in-laws had been good friends with the pastor, and they were part of a group who hadn't agreed with his departure. Some of their friends moved on to other churches, and Ryan's parents hadn't decided what they were going to do.

We tried out other churches in the area as well. Most of the time, I visited churches on my own first. I was fearful if Ryan had too many bad experiences with churches, it might turn him off for a while. Once again, we looked at Willow Creek's association of churches as a starting point. I visited Baptist, Methodist, Wesleyan, Congregational, and nondenominational churches, and each place offered up its own version of praises to Jesus.

It never once occurred to me to look beyond evangelicals for a home church. It's what my husband and I both knew. I like being evangelical. The doctrines in these churches, although differences do exist, overall line up with what we believe. Lord willing, if we had a child someday, I wanted her to have a similar church experience to mine. I wanted her to learn Bible stories in Sunday school, I wanted her to grow up singing praise and worship songs (with maybe a hymn or two thrown in for old time's sake), and I wanted her enrolled in an Awanas or Bible drills program. At this point, I wasn't looking for a new church tradition, I was looking for the same type of church I knew in a new town. All of these churches offered that in one way or another.

Visiting all these churches also gave me a lesson in communication. Often, these smaller churches didn't have a website, and I had a hard time determining what time their Sunday morning services even started.

One week, I determined I'd visit a Wesleyan church, not knowing a thing about the Wesleyans other than John Wesley was a good Christian man who had been a church leader a long time ago. I thought he started the Methodist denomination, but maybe he had a couple denomination start-ups under his belt. That was enough for me. I couldn't find the times for their worship service, so I called the church phone number. The phone rang a few times before being answered by the pastor of the church. After my initial surprise, we had a delightful conversation, and I told him we'd see him at church the following Sunday. I told Ryan about the exchange, and he decided to attend church with me that week.

The church was a few miles outside of town, a small, white wooden structure. The parking lot was even smaller, and there were maybe fifty people inside. I'm pretty sure we were the only guests that day, as the pastor came right up to us and asked me if I was the lady he'd spoken with on the phone. His wife led us in worship, and she had an amazing voice. The pastor gave a good sermon—although I don't remember the topic—using a white board. I could sense that, although this church wasn't big, it had a good pastoral team. My husband and I were both impressed with the quality of the service. My heartbeat accelerated a little, wondering if we'd found a church home—our second, my ninth. After the closing song, the pastor asked us to take a seat. His wife joined him up front, and they began thanking the congregation for all the support they'd shown them in the few years they'd been at the church. This would be their last Sunday in Michigan before making the move to the Carolinas. It was back to square one for us—again.

I hadn't met with success in visiting these small town churches, although I don't have anything bad to say about them. Often, these congregations are multiple generations of a few families who still meet together for worship. It can be hard for an outsider to fit in. Also, remember, I was trying to find a church that would meet all our needs: a place where I could serve, where my husband didn't feel surrounded by (perceived) weirdness, and where there was some kind of children's ministry as we hoped to have a child someday soon.

A family friend encouraged us to try Third Reformed church in Kalamazoo. I didn't know anything about the Reformed tradition, but she mentioned this church was a bigger one, and she knew people who attended there and liked it. Ryan and I visited one Sunday. I was about four months pregnant by this time, and was hopeful that, if we weren't going to sell our house and be moved into a new one by the time our baby arrived, we could at least worship together as a family at a church we called home. Third Reformed was huge. It was everything you'd expect a big, suburban evangelical church to be. Loud praise music with an excellent sound system. A dynamo pastor. Nothing was out of order in the fast-paced service. We liked our Sunday there, but hoped to find something smaller and in one of the towns we planned to live in someday. In the bulletin, there was a blurb about a church plant Third Reformed had recently started in a small town a few miles north. Currently, the congregation met in the town's middle school. The time and location were listed right there in Third's bulletin. We decided to try it the next Sunday.

At 10:30 in the morning that following Sunday, we drove up to the middle school, and saw large tent signs the church has put up temporarily on Sundays for ten years now. If there was ever a church that passed Ryan's parking lot test, this church did. There was a motorcycle or two parked in front. We saw about an equal number of large pickup trucks as SUVs and minivans. Not a necktie to be seen, even on the pastor. T-shirts, jeans, or shorts were the norm. The praise and worship band was a talented group. The pastor was dressed casually and an engaging speaker. Although it was a healthy mix of ages, there were plenty of young families, people roughly our age. We worshiped with North Point for the first time in August 2007, and have not stopped. We both knew the very first Sunday we went there, we'd found our next church home.

We didn't know a single person at the church. I take that back—I didn't know a single person. Being from the community, Ryan had a few teachers and friends of his parents who went there, but we only began to figure this out as we starting attending regularly. Since its beginning, members of the congregation have set up and torn down our "church" every Sunday. It's a thankless commitment for which I'm grateful. For years, if the cafeteria was being cleaned or set up for something else, we'd meet in the gymnasium instead (a large gym where our congregation would get lost sitting among the few bleachers pulled out and the rows of chairs set up). A couple times each year, we'd borrow the school's swimming pool to baptize new believers. Our babies were sprinkled in whatever cafeteria/gym we were using on a particular Sunday. We had access to several of the classrooms for our children's ministry. North Point had been meeting for about a year when we joined them. They were part of the Reformed Church of America (RCA), which meant nothing to me, but I had a suspicion it meant I was surrounded by people who had a Dutch heritage. I'd only lived in southwest Michigan for a year and a half, but I was learning that the Dutch had heavily populated the area. I'd find out later that my suspicions had been correct; parts of the Reformed tradition have its roots in the Netherlands.

It only took me a few sermons to realize these RCA people took their Bible seriously. Typically, Pastor Jason teaches a six-to-eight-week series on a topic. No matter where the key verses are for a particular message, we'd end up looking up passages all over the Bible by the end of the sermon. Over the years, he's delivered excellent sermons. I've saved downloaded versions of his sermons on the Jewish feasts, the Ten Commandments, and the Beatitudes, because they offered such new information to me. I can say without any doubt, I have grown more at North Point than I have at any other church in my life. Of course, many things correlate to this; the number of years I have been a Christian, spiritual growth through theological study, the teachings from my pastor, and increased Bible study.

That growth got its kickstart in the fall of 2007. I did the unthinkable—six months pregnant, I waddled up to the woman who had set up a women's ministry table in the lobby one Sunday morning and introduced myself. I say it's "unthinkable" tongue-in-cheek because things like this really don't bother me that much—she's my Christian *sister*, yes? Stop letting these things intimidate you. After telling her we were new in town and I had my days free, she encouraged me to visit their weekly Bible study. At that time, the group met at a local Scout house on Wednesday mornings. I went the next week, saying hello again to Karin, one of the teachers; meeting the other co-teacher, Karen, and a few other women. It was a small but welcoming group. By this point, I'd done several Bible studies with other groups of believers. Plus, I had my childhood experience with Bible drills and Bible quizzing. It can be very hard for me to join a new group like this and not appear to be a total Bible-loving dork. I've learned to live with it.

I loved our time of Bible study together each week. It ministered to me specifically at this time in my life, as we were still waiting to find our own home. I was more than ready to create community, even though we'd made little progress on selling our house, or finding a new one. These women would become my sisters who would pray for me as we tried to sell our home and find a new one over the next few years.

We had a baby girl in January 2008. She was only a few months old when changes occurred in Bible study. We moved the group to the home of another young mom, Jaime. My original Bible study teacher, Karen, went to work full-time, so Karin, the new women's ministry coordinator, took the helm (I'll trust you were able to follow that). Karin taught us for a few months at Jaime's house, but she didn't feel like Bible teaching was her gift. She asked me at some point if I would consider taking over the teaching portion. I agreed to do so, if someone would hold my little one when she wasn't taking her morning nap during Bible study. Trust me, there were several volunteers. Although God had prepared me in a thousand little ways, that "yes" opened up a whole new world of ministry for me.

I met a handful of women through Bible study, and even more from being a first-time mom in a church full of young moms. North Point was so new, I hadn't walked into someone's childhood church. People might know one another from being at other churches together in the past or from living in the same small towns, but it united us to do this church plant together. It was harder to feel like an outsider, because we were all new to North Point. Still, it took me a long time to meet people outside of my immediate mom-of-a-preschooler world. In the early days, the only people I knew were the children's minister, and those women I'd met through Bible study and play dates. One Sunday morning, I saw a lady a few years older than me come rushing up to two other ladies seated behind me. She had such a bright, sunny disposition, and I wondered how they knew one another. Over time, Sherry and I formed a friendship of our own, through our shared love of reading and Bible study. It just took time. Another instance, I served on a food committee for an upcoming church event. Margaret was also in this group. She radiated joy, and I longed to have a positive friend like that, who could share all her secrets of contentment with me. Today, Margaret is one of my favorite people on the planet, and a dear friend. She's simply Margaret, through and through. Seeing these women reminded me of all the women I'd been close to over the years in other churches. Women of all ages. In the early days, I wondered if I would ever have those kinds of connections at North Point.

Our God loves to do more than we can ask or imagine. By this point, my spiritual hunger was on overdrive. I'd gotten to know Pastor Jason better and we would exchange book titles from time to time. If I called him with a question about ministry, I had to make sure I had a decent amount of time to talk, because we chased all kinds of theological rabbit trails. I was reading new-to-me authors who were expanding my faith practices. Teaching Bible study added a whole new level of participation, and I spent a lot of time supplementing the material with my own research. I had an ever-deepening desire to know more about Jesus. One of my favorite things about Pastor Jason is he never minds if I email him questions about things I am thinking through—he claims to enjoy receiving these emails because they allow him to think on spiritual things rather than the daily tasks of operating a church.

In the midst of all this personal spiritual growth, Karin asked me to meet her at the public library one evening. At that meeting, she informed me she was stepping down as women's ministry leader. She'd prayed about it, and felt God leading her to ask me if I was interested in the position. Apparently, she'd also talked with Pastor Jason, and he was in agreement. I too prayed about the opportunity, and talked it over with my husband. In August 2010, I took on the role of women's ministry coordinator. This means I oversee the ministry efforts pertaining specifically to the women of our church. Bible studies, holiday dinners, social outings, special events, and occasional gifts on Mother's Day, Easter, and other holidays.

I thought I'd arrived at what God had been preparing me to do my whole life. He gave me a heart for the women of this church, who remain so dear to me. They are faithful and godly and willing to be known. Karin had started a women's ministry website, and I had written articles for it from time to time. I hadn't written creatively for years. It felt good. Better than that; it felt right.

Once I took on the role of women's ministry coordinator, I started writing more regularly on our ministry blog. At its peak, we had five weekly Bible studies going. The first women's event I planned was a night of line dancing in a barn (Southern Baptists here, there, and yonder got a good laugh out of that one). We've done all sorts of things in the years I've led this group of women. Mostly, what I've found is a group of women who are hungry for more of God. We did social events, as a way to get to know the women in this new church of ours, but it evolved into something deeper. Deep into God's word. Deep into studying theology. Deep into one another's lives. For the first time since I'd left my hometown, I'd found people my family could do life with—this group of women has buried loved ones, celebrated weddings and births, watched some leave our church, welcomed others into the fold. We created community.

The Reformed tradition baptizes infants, a visible sign and seal of joining a covenant community of believers. As our pastor often says, "making a big deal of God and his covenant promises." They will also baptize a new believer as an adult, but largely it's infant baptisms. Our pastor, so gifted at teaching, delivered a few sermons explaining why we baptized infants rather than dedicating them. He convinced me.. Our daughter was baptized at 14 months (it did take me a while to come around). I felt completely comfortable with our choice, until she turned seven, the age where I made my own personal profession of faith. I wondered if a second baptism was necessary now that she'd reached an age of decision. Again, I emailed Pastor Jason my concerns. The conversation was in-depth enough that it warranted a phone call. I am incredibly grateful for an accessible pastor. This is where I have landed. When we baptized our daughter as a baby, it brought her into a covenant relationship with God. We were proclaiming these covenant promises for her, and asking our family and the congregation to help us raise her up in the Lord. A second baptism wasn't necessary. That being said, I think believers can overthink baptism. My mom has been baptized twice in her life, and each one serves as a memory of various faith milestones for her. I won't abandon a brother or sister of the faith based on an opinion about baptism. What I've discovered about baptism is something I believe is true about many of our perceived differences in the church. Sprinkled, immersed, young, old, symbolic, covenantal, baptism should be a moment when an individual, or the parents and church on the individual's behalf, proclaims publicly they are serious about becoming a Christ-follower and serving their church. In those baptism waters, we acknowledge our belief that it is God, through his son's precious blood, that saves us. It's a sacrament of the church and is to be taken seriously. God knows the heart of the baptized. That's what he really wants—our heart.

I thought in every way I'd arrived. Learning more theology awakened a God-given part inside of me. The women's ministry events were well attended. I had great support from the leadership of our church. Identified as a church leader, I was asked to participate in worship by incorporating announcements into our service each week. Not only were announcements a new thing in our church, time on Sunday morning is considered precious. With a set number of worship songs and a 30- to 40-minute sermon, only a few minutes would be given to this new task. It was an honor to be entrusted with this role, and it was the first time I could remember seeing a woman speak from the stage in any church I'd attended.

In an effort to make even this time of the service meaningful, I worked with the worship leader on incorporating scripture, corporate prayers, and other liturgical pieces into the allotted time. Further, I enjoyed writing for our women's ministry blog so much, I began writing one of my own. It seemed obvious to me God had placed me in this church for such a time as this, and if anything were to change in this scenario, it would only be bigger and better.

Isn't it interesting how we convince ourselves we know exactly where our lives are headed? Sometimes, we think we have God all figured out.

For more than ten years now, Pastor Jason has been my pastor, longer than any other pastor. About year five of the church planting efforts (he'd been my pastor for four of those years), the church started hearing that Pastor Jason had gone on a vacation. He did take hunting and fishing trips from time to time, even going to the beaches of Florida when his wife could talk him into it, but this seemed more of an extended vacation of sorts. We had various guest speakers from our congregation, and one from the mother church that had started North Point. Finally, an elder stood before us one Sunday and let us know Pastor Jason had confided some personal struggles to our elders. Along with overseeing the doctrine of the church body, church discipline, and promotion of evangelism, the elder board's role was to provide pastoral care. In this case, it was our pastor who needed the care.

I would find out later, when I had a chance to speak with Pastor Jason myself, he'd come dangerously close to burning out. He'd been reading in a chair at his home one day when he became overwhelmed with fatigue. In his words, "I realized I had no desire to get up out of my chair. It's hard to describe, but I was completely zapped of all motivation. I didn't know if I could keep doing this."

Pastor Jason's story isn't unique. In some capacity, all of us who are passionate for the Lord will experience times of exhaustion—mentally, spiritually, physically. Church work is, well, a lot of work. We have to put spiritual practices in place that help us abide in Christ. It's essential to have close friends who know you and care about you beyond the ministry of the church. My pastor was at the end of his rope and thankfully our church leadership heard his cry for help.

Meet Aaron

I admire his writing, although his story leaves me sad. I read many blogs and inevitably come across some who have been deeply wounded by a church experience. Aaron has been hurt by the church, but he writes about it with grace. There's such a hunger for Jesus and community in his words. I pray for him, that he would find the right community for him and his family.

I grew up in the hallowed pews.

I don't remember a time before church. My Sunday mornings were filled with songs, stories, teaching, and preaching. I grew up around psalmists, pastors, and prophets. This is what it meant to be a charismatic, from banners on the church walls to the tongues at prayer meetings. Everyone had an anointing of some kind, some sort of supernatural calling on his or her life that gave them authority. I was surrounded by *Charisma* magazines, stories of faith healers, and Christian AM radio. I knew the end of the world was coming, all we had to do was see the signs. I was sure, on most days, I would be one of the faithful raptured away from this earth before everything burned.

This was growing up a dispensational charismatic.

At the same time, I attended an Episcopal school. The contrast with my charismatic, nondenominational Sunday mornings was striking. In school chapel I learned to genuflect. On Sunday mornings I learned how to dance and sing in the Spirit. In school I learned from Father Bob about saints and feast days and saying the collects. On Sundays I learned from Pastor Dave about verse by verse exposition, historical biblical events, and how this applied and translated into today.

In a lot of ways, I was lucky growing up. I had good teachers who loved Jesus and cared about the sheep entrusted to their care. Even with the weird theology I inherited, some of it quite dangerous, I still have fond memories of growing up in the church.

After high school, I was on my own. The church of my youth had dissolved and I had nowhere to go. So I went church shopping for the first time.

I ended up at an Evangelical Free church, where I promptly became enmeshed with the youth group. This was where I bloomed as a young Christian. Here I learned to preach, to teach, to lead. Here I committed myself to Jesus in ways I was unable to as a kid. My love for the church grew with my love for Jesus. I discovered I had a heart for discipleship, for helping other people understand the Bible, and for developing a robust theology of my own.

The story is not all idealistic though. It was at this Evangelical Free church I first discovered the barbs of believers. Here I was hurt, deeply. Here I was overlooked. Here I was first wounded by the church. The validity of my salvation was questioned on more than one occasion. I was judged by my failings. I had to fight to prove myself worthy of leadership in the eyes of gatekeepers.

It wasn't all one sided. I hurt many people during my early twenties. I have many regrets, many things I wish I could do over, many people I wish I could say sorry to.

We're not good at this. The church doesn't do well with conflict. When feelings are hurt, and we grow weary of fighting for the cause of Christ within the walls of a certain church, it's all too easy to move on down the road to another church. Or worse, to leave the church altogether.

When I left the church, it was on good terms, but no one missed me. No one came to find me. No one seemed to care that I had moved on. But seasons change, and the Spirit leads, opening doors and closing others. I took an opportunity to become music leader for a Christian Missionary Alliance church plant. Here I learned the power of song and liturgy. Here my dreams of what church could be got a little room to manifest. I discovered and wrote songs to lead the congregation to the table of Jesus and catch a vision of what it meant to be a Christian.

I sang every week and continued to teach on most Friday nights. After a year and a half of this (on top of my five years prior teaching at least once a week every week), I was burned out to say the least. Six years of nonstop preparation. Six years of dedicating my life to the mission of the church. Six years of investment. I stepped down from my music leader position for a while, and just like that I wasn't part of the congregation

> anymore. Once again, no one came to check on me. No one came looking for me. The pastor I worked hard beside didn't say a word of encouragement to me. Once again I was left alone.

Hear the frustration. The disillusionment. These things can leave us feeling frightfully alone and altogether unheard.

> Is it a wonder I feel like the church's abused mistress, kept near as long as I am willing to give of myself but forgotten when it comes to my needs? See, through those six years I worked in, for, and with the church, I showed different signs I needed help. Mania, depression, cyclical actions that were just chalked up to sin. No one urged me to look into therapy. No one urged me to talk to my doctor. As long as I was giving of my time, talents, and treasures, I was kept around no matter how self-destructive I was. But, as soon as I needed from the community, I found myself alone in the whistling wind.
>
> I tried to get back into church life. I volunteered my time and talents again to a church after I moved from Utah to Oregon. But it was the same story. When I took a step backward from community, no one took that step with me. I was alone again.
>
> So, now I'm in this spiritual wilderness. I'm in a place that should be lonely, desolate, bereft of community, yet I'm finding community here. There are a lot of us outside the church walls, a lot of us hurt and burned and wounded by the church. And while we are weary and wary of the church, we love Jesus and each other. We come together in houses, coffeeshops, bars, and online. We might be misfits, but at least out here in the wild wilderness we are accepted for who we are. Questions, doubts, wounds, and anger are welcome in our various loose-knit congregations.
>
> And we are congregations; with teachers, preachers, music makers, and prophets. See, the Spirit is moving among the margins, the ragtag, the broken, and the brave. We love these

> churches we are creating, finding, and being found in. There are no pews to fill, so no one cares about a head count. No one cares about the finances, because there is no institution to uphold and keep the lights on.
>
> In this wilderness, I'm finding a new chapter of my church story. I'm discovering I still love church, even the churches that left me so alone. I'm discovering that spiritual health, healing, and hope are possible. I'm discovering that even though I may be done with traditional church, Jesus isn't done with me.
>
> So maybe this isn't a church story; maybe this is a Spirit story. We have yet to see the ending, so who's to say what could happen. But if the Spirit is breathing life into these pages, then this is a story ultimately about redemption and resurrection. Who knows what form that will take? All I know is the history doesn't write my future, yet it has shaped me. I am who I am—good, bad, wounded, and cynical—because of the churches I grew up in. My spirituality is an amalgamation of the traditions I have swum in, which ultimately has led me to a singular focus on Jesus.
>
> The Jesus I met in the churches of my youth is the same Jesus who meets me in this spiritual wilderness. Jesus is the one who has formed and filled me. Jesus is the one who leads me, saves me, calls me. The Jesus I asked into my heart as a child is the same Jesus who I gave my on-fire heart to in my early twenties, and is the same Jesus I entrust my broken heart to now.

For Pastor Jason, our elders told this man who hesitated to take any time off, they wanted him to leave his pastoral responsibilities completely for a month. It wasn't up for negotiation. He took a trip out west and we were instructed to not contact him about anything. I thought to myself, "Our poor pastors. What do we do to them?"

I'd been here before, experiencing the fall of a pastor. Except this time felt different. I wasn't experiencing it as a child, or a casual church attendee. I was in leadership with this pastor, and I hadn't seen it coming. Jason is a major extrovert, full of passion and energy.

If he's at risk for burning out, it can certainly happen to any of us. Under the leadership of wise elders, our church did right by our pastor. Mandatory paid time off, focused prayer for our pastor, and a whole slew of well wishes (you didn't really think we wouldn't contact him in any way for a whole month, did you)? I don't honestly know how many people infringed on his privacy during his time away but the relationship we have with our pastors is such a tender one. I gave it a week or two but then had to shoot him a quick text, "Are you OK?" It's always a fine line between desperately needing that personal space but wanting to be missed. Pastor Jason was able to make some much-needed adjustments in his personal and professional life, going on to serve our congregation even better than he had before his time away.

Pastor Jason has his preaching idiosyncrasies too, just like my college pastor, Dr. Marshall, did. He too likes the word *therefore*, but instead of saying "when you see *therefore* in scripture, you'd better see what it's there for" like Dr. Marshall did, Pastor Jason would stop and emphasize the word *therefore* when we would come to it. He'd say it *gangster style*. Imagine how Mr. T would say it. Say it out loud one time yourself. Now you know.

Pastor Jason likes Slinkies and the GI Joe figurines with a kung fu grip. He's told us often he was taught as a child that roller-skating leads to sex. He was kidding, sort of. He's an educated, smart preacher, with more than a touch of backwoods. Another word he always emphasizes when we see it in scripture is the word *but*. He tells us to always pay attention to what happened before and after the *but* because it will usually show us what God is up to in the story.

That's what I'm learning still. As I said, I convinced myself I'd always be in leadership at North Point Church, a member of the Reformed Church of America. Pastor Jason tells me I'm still quite Baptist, but I learned the Dutch acronym TULIP along the way, and I think I could persuade you that I believe almost all of its points, not just two or three. But. God had more for me than a leadership position in one church in one faith tradition. I just didn't know it yet.

Chapter 6

My Daughter's Church

About the time our daughter's little legs started hanging well past her booster seat, we were running errands in town one day. We drove by a Wesleyan church, and she said, "Mom, there's our Bible study church." She was right. Since North Point doesn't have a building, we've had to find different locations to house our weekday events. Friendship Wesleyan has been the home of our women's Bible study on Wednesday mornings for several years. When our daughter was a baby, I heard about a local church who offered a Sisters of Motherhood group (similar to the national organization MOPS, Mothers of Preschoolers). We attended that group at the Baptist Church (not SBC) until I sent her off to kindergarten. A few times, we hosted mother/daughter events on a Saturday, and the Church of God church opened up its doors for us. We partnered with the Congregational church for VBS. In my own ministry life, where God was doing many new things, he was doing an old but beautiful thing in the life of my daughter. She was learning what I had learned as a child—you can find Jesus in many churches. I don't want her growing up with a bunch of biases, and it occurred to me we were well on our way.

She has attended one church her entire life. Alyssa, Heidi, Sawyer, they were all there in the nursery together from infancy. I'm thankful for the foundation that has set for her. At home, though, we spend a lot of time talking about how other Christians do things. I don't want her to grow up thinking ours is the only way, or even the right way. It's important to me she realizes other Christians don't do things wrong necessarily, but in a way foreign to her. Most of all, I don't want her to be intimidated when she enters a church where worship incorporates formal liturgy, or one where they spread themselves throughout the church so they can speak in tongues, jump up and down, maybe even wave flags and tap tambourines. Much like the song we taught her as a toddler: "Jesus loves the little children; red and yellow, black and white, they are precious in his sight." What if we added another verse? "Jesus loves the little children; Pentecostals, Catholics, Mennonites, they are precious in his sight." Although it might take more effort to make it work rhythmically. I don't know, I came pretty close there. You get the idea.

I have taken my daughter on parts of this faith journey with me. She went with me to the Methodist church in our small village one Sunday. I don't recall why we didn't attend our own church that morning, but this particular day, she and I went somewhere else. They were set up for communion. The homemade bread, baked by one of the women in the church, was placed under a linen cloth. The pitcher of grape juice sat beside it. Before the service, I explained those elements to her. At our own church, the kids go off to class after the worship songs, so they don't see adults take communion. Also, I hadn't made a clear choice on when she could participate in communion. She'd been baptized at the age of one, and likely would not have a believer's baptism. That left it unclear, in my mind, when she should participate in communion. I'd talked with a friend whose father is a conservative pastor, and she remembered not taking communion until she was a teenager. Her father had wanted to make sure she understood the magnitude of what she was choosing to participate in at the table. Meanwhile, other faith traditions, like Lutherans and Catholics, have a set age when they lead their children through classes preparing them for First Communion. It's a big deal. And for Episcopalians and others, all baptized Christians are welcome at the table, regardless of age. Who among us truly understands the mystery of communion, after all?

Where did I fall in my belief system right at that moment? This was one example of a time when I offered lip service to how open I was in learning about the various ways Christians observed their faith but what would I choose to do when it came time to put it to action in my own personal life? Did I think there was a wrong decision to make here, seated before a communion table where my daughter could, technically, participate? She had no believer's baptism, no immersion in a baptistry, yet she had been baptized. She'd prayed the sinner's prayer with me on more than one occasion. I could see evidence of the Holy Spirit influencing her decision making more all the time.

I made my choice. I told her if she wanted to go up with Mom that morning and take communion, she could. Step by step, I explained to her what would happen. She was a little nervous, but wanted to participate. A friend attends this church, and she always makes it a point to greet me when I visit. It's such a welcoming thing to look around a roomful of strangers, and know she's glad I'm there. She smiled at me knowingly, from one mom to another, when my little girl stepped out into the aisle. I watched my daughter first take the bread, *body of Christ, broken for you*, dip it in the juice, *blood of Christ poured out for you*, and quietly return to the pew. I'll never forget this first as long as I live. To this day, communion is a big deal to her. I don't know if she fully understands the significance of what we're doing, I certainly don't, but she knows it's important. In our own church, on the third Sunday of every month, we take communion and elders go around to the children's classrooms to let the teachers take the elements. Every time, she asks me either to come get her for communion, or let her teacher know it's all right if she partakes. Just last Sunday she leaned over to me during the singing and whispered, "Mom, I wish every week was communion Sunday." She knows communion is something she's privileged to be a part of, and I'm excited this is one of many steps she'll take to make her faith her own.

Meet Rhonda

From my childhood home, you'd go down the gravel road, turn right, and she lived at the end of that second dirt road. She was one of my closest friends, and she's Catholic. I value her perspective as I strive to learn more about this faith tradition. Here, she shares about her experience as a "cradle Catholic," who has passed down the ancient traditions of Catholicism to her children:

> Growing up Catholic is a wonderful gift my mother gave me. She came from a very devout Catholic family, even graduating from an all-girls Catholic high school in Illinois. When I started my family, I couldn't wait to give them that gift. As a cradle Catholic, I grew up with the traditions and rituals, and never gave them much thought until I started my own family. I wanted to be able to explain to them, not so much why we believe what we believe, because I feel that is somewhat evident, but more so why we do what we do. Every ritual and tradition within the church has a deep meaning to it. From simpler things like the sign of the cross to more spiritual things like going to confession. Even though my mom died when I was fifteen, I had learned a lot from her, and she had instilled in me the gift and importance of faith. Still, I was at a loss at not being able to talk with her and gain that important knowledge once I was coming of age as a mother myself, and doing more wondering.
>
> Rather than ask my mother these important questions, I attended Rite of Christian Initiation of Adults (RCIA) classes as much as possible, read a lot of books on our faith tradition, and asked questions of my priest. The process led me to discover a great deal more about the beautiful gift I had been given by my mother and grandparents. It made me excited to give that gift to my children.
>
> First Communion is always a huge milestone for a young Catholic. The child, starting around second grade, is better able

> to understand what he is receiving than he would be at a younger age. Even at that age and older, it is still hard to communicate to our children what a great joy, privilege, and especially duty it is to receive the Eucharist. My children never had many questions about the beliefs and traditions, because their catechism classes were good about preparing them. Each child has to meet with the priest before the "big day," and be able to discuss what he or she has learned. As part of First Communion, children attend confession and do penance. My kids were all scared of this part. As a child, I remember being nervous as well. I didn't want to have to tell the priest sinful things I had done. As I prepared my own children for this first time, it was rather fun to chat with them about my experience, and help them be less nervous. The day of each child's First Communion was a huge day of celebration, both at church and at home. We hosted a dinner and a reception. These are days I'll always remember.

This is so much of what I want for our own daughter, although we are not raising her Catholic. I want her to remember major milestones in her faith. I want her to be comfortable coming to me with questions, and expressing where she is with her faith. I want to join her in celebrating her faith, as she claims more and more of it on her own. Finally, I want her to know she has a place at this big, expansive table. We don't all practice our faith the exact same way, but our God is big enough to embrace all the ways we encounter Jesus. And Jesus sits at the head of the table. Always.

We took a trip to St. Louis last year, at the beginning of the Lenten season. We arrived in town on Ash Wednesday, with about forty-five minutes to spare before Mass was scheduled to begin at the old cathedral downtown. Sitting in our pew, I explained to her what she could expect during the service, as best as I could recall. I'd only been to an Ash Wednesday service once myself. She seemed interested in going, but was concerned about leaving the ash markings in the form of a cross on her forehead after we left the church. I told her I didn't think it mattered if she wiped them off before she left.

As we entered the majestic cathedral, I internally squealed with delight. Our girl has grown up in a church plant that meets in a middle school. We call our sanctuary the cafetorium, for obvious reasons; during the week, it's a cafeteria. Here she is, learning about a whole other way of doing church. Behold the beauty of a cathedral that's well over a hundred years old. Honoring God by making the building where you worship beautiful, not just functional. And is it ever beautiful. The statues around the room show the Holy Family, and saints gone before us. There's a statue of Mary, with a stand of lit candles in front of her image. Our little girl knows to dip her hands in the holy water, making the sign of the cross before her. Another thing she recognizes as a big deal. She thrills at doing this almost as much as her mom does.

We arrived early, so there were only a few other people in the room. Again, right away, I noticed the silence, a lost art in our evangelical worship. She flipped the prayer kneeler down, kneeling to pray for a few minutes. Then, as I'm sure thousands of other young believers have done across the generations, she couldn't resist flipping it up and down on repeat a few times. I nudged her to quiet down and stop playing with the kneeler.

With only a few minutes before the liturgy began, the sanctuary was mostly full. When the time came to step out into the aisle, she walked in front of me, making her way to the priest. I love that Ash Wednesday is for everyone. I think it points to a union the church longs for. I'm thankful, so thankful, she gets to hear these words, too. *Remember that you are dust, and to dust you shall return.* Like me, like you, she's part of an eternal tradition of sinners becoming saints, thanks to the precious blood of Christ. The moment we made it back to our hotel room, she went into the bathroom, grabbed a Kleenex, and wiped any remaining ash from her forehead.

Inviting people to explore other churches with you doesn't always go smoothly. It's one thing to show up for a service at the wrong time or sit through a Mass wondering what it is exactly they're doing when you're on your own (I have done both). When you include someone else, though, you want it to go well and add meaning to his or her life. I searched online for a stations of the cross service for my daughter and me to attend one Lenten season. We'd been together before, and she'd paid attention the whole time. Moving around the nave from station to station helped. I found a Catholic church by us in the country that had a service right after school. We arrived at the same time as several families did, which meant the time listed online had been correct. So far, so good. When we got inside, we found the holy water, flipped down our kneelers, and spent a few minutes in silence. Dare I say we looked like we knew what we were doing? Pride goeth before the fall. The service began, and I noticed we never made our way to the first station. Sort of strange, but Catholic services don't follow the exact same format in my experience, so I was patient with the singing, and the reading of verses. Still no movement toward the framed plaques on the walls surrounding the church. The last stations of the cross service we'd went to had been at an Episcopal church, so maybe that was the difference.

The service went on for more than an hour. They started to reveal the cross in stages out from under a cloth. Kind of meaningful, I thought. Then, the congregation stood and started making their way to the cross. They'd kneel (genuflect) and kiss (venerate) it. I learned the terms in parentheses after I got home and googled what we had seen. With growing hesitation, my daughter looked at me. By this time, I had visited several churches and the cardinal rule seemed to be this; don't stand out. I whispered to her we'd go up there, but she didn't have to kiss the cross. What on earth? We could touch the cross. Surely that would be acceptable? So we did. We took our place in line, and when it came our turn, my daughter reached out with one finger and rapidly did a quick tap on the cross, before practically running back to her seat. I followed suit. The service ended shortly thereafter. Apparently, I had gotten the times wrong that day, and we attended a Veneration of the Cross liturgy. A service like this one has taken place in churches dating back to at least the sixth century. Of course, this was not something we did in my evangelical circles. In my head, I would have been convinced it bordered on idolatry. My heart these days was much less certain.

Oh, by the way, the stations of the cross service would take place later that evening. We did not return for that service.

Our church recently incorporated a program where our teens can learn the basic tenets of the Reformed tradition. For some of you, images of catechism or confirmation classes or those leading up to a Bar Mitzvah are flashing before you. Rather than attend a weekly class, this program is done at home as a family. After a group of kids goes through this class, they'll be presented to our consistory, deacons, and elders, and briefly interviewed as candidates for church membership. In a few short months, we'll begin this process with our daughter. Along with that, I plan on hosting an evening with our daughter and the women in our church who have mentored her over the years. I envision pouring affirmation and grace upon her as each woman speaks into her life.

Since we made the decision to baptize our daughter as a baby, one of the things that concerned me was what she would have to look back on as milestones of her faith. It's a common phrase I've come across, "remember your baptism," but those who are baptized as infants won't remember the event itself.

I attended my first Easter Vigil this past spring. It was at a local Catholic church I was familiar with and this time it didn't make me nervous to enter those doors (it gets easier every time). When I mentioned on Twitter I'd be attending my first vigil, one person told me not to get too wet. I had no idea what he was talking about. Well, at one point during the service, the priest walks around the entire nave area, sprinkling water from an aspergillum, over all the congregants. Why? To encourage all of us to "remember our baptism."

First, I've learned that phrase is bigger than an actual memory of the day of your baptism. It means remember what you are born into, and who has called you unto him. Secondly, I realize now there are other milestones my daughter can point to as she grows older. She'll have mountaintop spiritual experiences at church camp. I'm expectant that youth group will have a big impact. Then there's the variety of services she tries out with her mom. There are times she'll experience sadness or grief, and learn to take these things to God in prayer. We make a big deal of Advent, Lent, and Pentecost, as well as Christmas and Easter.

No, she's not always by my side when I learn about these new ways of worshiping Jesus. Our church hosted more traditional Holy Week services this year but because of commitments to a school activity, she wasn't able to attend. It's especially thrilling for me to think of bringing a variety of worship practices into our own church walls. Certainly, you don't always have to step outside your church to explore these new things. Bring them to your own fellowship as well. Invite a group in or learn to offer some of these rich historical Christian practices yourself. Regardless of where you do these new things, remember we're doing them to learn more about worshiping Jesus. A brother or sister in Christ who is interested in that should always be welcomed, in their own church or any church they visit.

Are we doing our children a disservice when we raise them in a "church bubble"? When I consider questions like this, I think of the varied believers I've met online. Several have a story similar to mine, evangelicals who knew nothing of the ancient practices of our faith. Others left behind the ancient traditions in search of a "personal relationship" with Jesus, and a tradition more focused on Bible study. All are my Christian brothers and sisters. Back and forth we go.

Meet Ed

> When I began to visit a Baptist church on Sundays, the Catholic priests at my home parish and at my Catholic high school would have none of it. They warned my family against the dangers of this Baptist church, discouraged me from reading the Bible on my own, and dismissed my questions with a smug all-knowing assurance.
>
> Little did they know that I had spent the past three years amassing an arsenal of Bible verses to use against the priests with my hidden NIV Bible and a drawer of yellow highlighters. When my mother's side of the family told me to obey the priests and to be "100% Catholic," I knew what my answer would be. I had known it for years.

The priests, my family, and many of my high school friends were deeply unsettled with my choice to become a Baptist. From their viewpoint, I had abandoned the one true church. From my own, I had been willing to straddle the two traditions for as long as necessary and had only made my choice under duress. While my Baptist church encouraged the exploration of the Bible, in my opinion the priests had overextended their authority and tried to rule with a heavy hand rather than encouraging curiosity and engagement.

Fifteen years later, my disillusionment with the Catholic authority system was rivaled by my despair over the lack of spiritual substance in the evangelical movement. I had given much of my life to knowing my faith, earning a bachelor's degree in Biblical literature at a Christian university, and then working my way through seminary for a Master of Divinity. By the time I was finished, I felt that I had primarily "mastered" what I didn't believe. I felt distant from God, if God even existed.

It took a pastor from one of my classes to give me my first nudge back to the Catholic tradition. At the time, I didn't know exactly what I was getting myself into. He invited me to a different kind of service that would be quiet and contemplative. We sang chants, lit candles, repeated the Jesus Prayer, and sat in silence. I felt distant from God, uncertain about my beliefs, and unsure about what it looked like to practice my faith day in, day out. Cramming my mind with Bible verses and doctrine did little to bridge the divide I perceived between myself and God. Would this church service finally break through?

The short answer is no, it absolutely did not. I approached the service expecting a miracle, an epiphany, or a mountaintop transfiguration of sorts. While this service sparked greater curiosity on my part about the prayers I had stumbled through, I hardly found the link to God I had sought.

By God's mercy, I began to attend a Vineyard church several years later where our pastors regularly practiced contemplative prayer and graciously helped fill in some of the important gaps I had been missing. While I had some idea about the music and intercessory prayer that played key roles in our Sunday services, I also had opportunities to learn from contemplative teachers about the slow transformation that occurs through contemplative prayer. Along the way, these teachers from the Vineyard movement began to recommend books on contemplative prayer—even books by Catholic writers.

While my evangelical university had introduced us to a few Catholic writers such as Henrí Nouwen and Brennan Manning (our second son is named after him, in fact), I had unfortunately never considered that Catholic writers could teach me about prayer. As it turned out, the lack of spiritual instruction and the missing daily spiritual practices in my evangelical tradition were all waiting for me in the pages of these Catholic writers. They prepared me to read books by Richard Rohr and Thomas Merton, among other contemporary Catholic authors of spiritual books.

After moving away from the city with the Vineyard church, we now attend an Episcopal church in our small Kentucky town. The incense is unbearable, the robes look weird, and I literally know zero songs in our hymnal. It's not ideal at times. On the other hand, each service includes time for silent contemplative reflection, the sermons are short but edifying, our priest regularly invites me to teach Sunday school classes on contemplation, and our coffee hour sandwiches are the stuff of legends.

This isn't the church I could have imagined for myself when I was highlighting Bible verses as a young teen. The good news is I am now part of a church that is grounded in the contemplative prayer tradition, a tradition that dates back to the earliest days of the church and has endured the test of time. When I wait in silence before the Lord, consenting to his loving presence, whether at home or at church, I feel that I am finally where I belong.

In all kinds of ways, I can see where my passion for learning from other believers is influencing my daughter's faith too. We have a growing collection of children's books to teach her about other ways of worship. These aren't easy to come by in our evangelical circles, but I always get a copy for our bookshelves when I read about them. From her collection, she's learned about what Catholic children are taught to do during Lent. She's also learned about Advent, Pascha, and a Sunday morning in an African American church. We've grown quite fond of a series of books about the Pope's fictitious cat, Margaret.

There are so many books I wish existed that I haven't found yet. If I'm being completely honest, sometimes I feel cheated by the faith of my childhood. It was life-giving in many ways, but I didn't learn anything about church history or ancient traditions. Traditions that are Christian, not just Catholic. Crossing oneself, ancient prayers, anointing the sick, confessing our sins to one another, lamenting . . . these acts are part of our heritage too, and can add a richness to one's faith. I want my daughter to have an awareness of these things. More than that, I want her to give them a try, and see them as excellent tools in deepening her faith.

I found a book on the saints once and I determined to read through it with her starting on All Saints' Day (November 1st). For years, I couldn't have told you the name of a single saint, except St. Patrick, the reason I wear green on March 17th. Ahem. We read through two or three pages in the book, and she asked, "Mom, will you please put that book in a garage sale? It's scary because all those people died."

While that attempt didn't go too well, I'm serious about teaching her these things, even if I do it clumsily. If you think churches fighting among themselves is new, you know as much about church history as I once did. We've been arguing over doctrine from the beginning. Church history is fascinating, and I'm always on the lookout for age-appropriate books to introduce her to these types of things. I've recently started praying the Liturgy of the Hours. This ancient tradition dates back to the days of the Old Testament. Every day, millions of Christians stop their busy lives and pray formally two to seven times a day. They pray the Lord's Prayer, the psalms, and some ancient and well-known prayers using one of several prayer books or downloading an app. It's not just a practice for monks, nuns, and priests. Christians of all traditions benefit from intentionally creating time in their day to stop and center their attention on God. I'm already seeing a difference in my levels of peace and groundedness as I learn this spiritual discipline, which takes me less than ten minutes. It can be confusing at times, and chances are good I'm technically doing it wrong. I'm a Protest-ant after all, used to doing it my way.

My Coptic Orthodox prayer book, *The Agpia*, a gift from a friend you'll hear from in the next chapter, has gotten my daughter curious. She's asked me what I'm doing and what it says. How could I adequately describe what I was encountering? That praying these words first thing in the morning felt like I started each day with the holiest of breaths? "In the name of the Father, and the Son, and the Holy Spirit, one God. Amen. Kyrie eleison, Lord have mercy, Lord have mercy, Lord bless us. Amen. Glory be to the Father, and to the Son, and to the Holy Spirit, both now and ever and unto the ages of ages. Amen."

Author Scot McKnight, in the book *Praying with the Church: Following Jesus Daily, Hourly, Today,* suggests a prayer called "The Jesus Creed." There's a student version of this book but I can also see the following words in a board book with beautiful illustrations: "'Hear, O Israel, the Lord our God, the Lord is one. Love the Lord your God with all your heart, with all your soul, with all your mind, and with all your strength.' The second is this: 'Love your neighbor as yourself.' There is no commandment greater than these." Include the Lord's Prayer, a morning and nighttime prayer, and you're on your way to developing a prayer warrior for the church.

While it can take a little digging for an evangelical parent like myself, there are prayer books for our children, and also books on what is going on during formal church liturgy, how to identify Christ in the Eucharist, what it means to observe the various seasons of the church calendar, and so forth.

I've also learned, in addition to our girl participating in other spiritual practices, it's important for her to simply see me living out my faith—maybe even more important. For years now, I've started my mornings by reading a passage out of a chronological Bible. I facilitate a group on Facebook that reads the Bible this way annually, so it often takes me thirty minutes or more to read the passage, research findings from that day's reading, and post insights on the Facebook group page. Our daughter has learned this is my time. If she's hungry, she'll get herself something to hold her over until I make breakfast. She'll ask me from time to time about what stories I read on a particular day. If she has learned one thing about her mama, it's that I spend a lot of time in God's word. She has her own chronological Bible, a graphic illustrated version called *The Action Bible.* This Bible doesn't go light on detail. We've read through it with her entirely once, and from time to time she'll sit with it on her own and read again. Daily habits are forming, with God's help.

Another way I've tried to be intentional about training up my daughter in the faith is making sure she is mentored by other people in the faith. There will likely come a time when she won't attend the same church as us, and I want her to know intrinsically, as I did, churches have God's people in them. I want her to believe this, even though they might not be the loudest voices or demand the greatest presence.

She has befriended Naomi, Marissa, Scott, Michael, Mark, Rebecca, Bailey, Dana, and her daughter Marlee. Some of these men and women have spent time in our home, while others are a regular fixture to her on Sunday mornings. They have been her Sunday school teachers, parents of her friends, but more importantly, they are the people she sees living out their faith. They are right there, a few rows over most Sundays, and without using any words, they teach her church is a big part of their life. At home, I'll give her updates on what these people have going on in their own life. She knows times they've moved, lost family members, or celebrated successes. She's learning church functions best as a spiritual family.

My daughter is forging a relationship with Jesus in her own way. She's on her own journey, but I want her to learn about the saints all around her who are traveling this narrow road home. I'd be delighted if we could continue attending the same church together for our whole lives. We go to church with my husband's parents and it's been nice to serve in various ministries together, attend events, sit by one another on Sunday morning and maybe enjoy a meal together afterward. Many weeks it's the only time we see each other. If there's one thing I've learned about church though, it's that circumstances change. I don't know if my daughter will always worship with Reformed Christians. Whatever churches she chooses to worship with someday, I hope we've given her enough experiences to not feel like she's entering unknown territory when she does so. I want her to attend a church where she is challenged. Where her faith can grow. I want her daily time with God to leave her face glowing as if she's been in his very presence. I want her to find a home church but also to love her Christian brothers and sisters worldwide. Most of all, I hope we've taught her different doesn't equate with wrong.

Chapter 7

More Wandering to Do

Meet Nicole

She's a writer friend of mine. We've only met in person a few times, but every encounter through our writings and actual conversation shows me we are soul sisters. Our stories vary, but our hearts, like so many I've met over the years, cry out for the same thing: more of Jesus. She became a Christian in high school, and spent her early days as a believer with the Southern Baptists. She encountered a tradition seemingly so certain about every aspect of their faith. She didn't give much thought to other ways of worshiping Jesus, until she saw more.

> I felt like I was discovering a whole new world as I held a green leather Book of Common Prayer, a gift from my Episcopal boyfriend. I discovered something that wasn't new at all—the rich ancient traditions my faith was built on. It felt like everything changed as I knelt in the pew, crossed myself at the altar, took communion from the hands of a female priest, sang the doxology.

Nicole's journey for more has taken her around the world. Isn't that exciting? She continues to discover the beauty of a God who is much more than one tradition could possibly express.

> Working in the ministry and nonprofit worlds over the past fifteen years, I have celebrated God from the back of a truck, rushing past lush rice fields, and I have sung the Daily Office with

> Cistercian monks from around the world. I have worshiped to the drums of South Asian believers sitting cross-legged on the floor, dusty, colorful, and full of life in one of the poorest slums on earth. I have marveled with thousands at God's beauty in one of the largest Middle Eastern churches, hewn from the side of a mountain that local believers say God literally moved to show his might. I have prayed from the dusty streets of an ancient city where some of the darkest evil of terrorism has been born and threatens this world, but cannot overcome it.

What I'm here to suggest in our final chapter together is this: attend a church expecting to find community and always, always, more of Jesus. When we attended Christ the King, Pastor Bob would often say, "If you find a perfect church, you'd better leave before you mess it up." I believe with my whole heart that when it comes to doing church, many, many of us are called to stay where we are. Not because we've found the perfect tradition, but because through those of us who are hungry for more, churches can find ways to come together and learn how to encounter Jesus using practices they never have used before.

In the conversations I have with people about learning new spiritual disciplines and exploring other Christian traditions, I typically get one of two responses. A person might whisper to me, looking around to make sure no one else is listening, "I'd like to explore that, but I don't want to try it alone." Maybe it seems too Catholic or too charismatic. There's an unwritten code surrounding many of our faith practices, that if you're not a part of that particular tradition, certain things might seem forbidden. I have not found this to be the case at all.

The second reaction I get is a proverbial turning of the head. "Nah, my faith is good the way it is." To which I would ask, when is the last time you really grew in your faith? The older I get, I realize living out one's faith is a holy marathon. That doesn't mean it has to be boring. Does your faith excite you? Are you passionate in your pursuit of Jesus? I'm not telling you that how you're doing faith is wrong. I'm telling you what I've found. There's more. Exploring new spiritual practices has opened my eyes to so many beautiful things. These fresh perspectives point to Jesus. More of Jesus.

While North Point Church has been a wonderful experience, and I have grown in my time there, it's not perfect. Over time, the women's ministry events weren't as well attended. I had a few women of great importance to me break fellowship, moving their membership to other churches. No, the break in fellowship wasn't required. They are always and forever my Christian sisters. Relationships change when you don't see one another at least once a week though. The conversations you used to have about church don't work anymore because people come and go and before long, they won't know the names you mention. Meanwhile, occasionally I still glance at "their place" in the sanctuary, and I remember how things used to be.

Our church hired a community coordinator, and it was decided she should be the person to deliver weekly announcements during worship services. I told myself I didn't mind, but sometimes I did. As time went on, I'd started to realize announcements could be a meaningful part of worship too. In my brief time on the stage I looked for liturgical pieces that would aid in the overall worship experiences. A prayer for certain times of the church calendar year, responsive readings, moments of silent prayer, intermingling spoken words with the beginning chords of praise songs. There's not an emphasis on these things now. I'm not disappointed I was asked to stop giving announcements. I'm saddened because I thought I was part of something other than updates on upcoming events.

In talking about this with others more familiar with the Reformed tradition, I have learned our own tradition has a history of formal liturgy. My church is decidedly contemporary in our style of worship, but in the tradition's past, the creeds, responsive readings, formal prayers were there. My Methodist pastor friend Andrew is married to a doctoral candidate Episcopalian who teaches at a local Reformed seminary. Did you follow that? Imagine the conversations around their dinner table. He mentioned to me they attend the seminary's chapel service on Fridays. They've extended an invitation for me to join them so I can experience firsthand the respect my own tradition has for formal liturgy. And yes, I certainly hope to bring some of those ideas back to my own church.

We're a young church, our hearts are seeking God; perhaps the role I thought God had for me is further down the road.

Bible study continues to flourish though. We have a handful of groups that meet each week. Our Wednesday night group has anywhere from eight to twenty-five in a given session. We've studied several books of the Bible in their entirety. We've read a variety of other books, as well. Sometimes we do a study with a DVD of the speaker, other times we make our way through a workbook on our own. A friend of mine began reading the Bible chronologically each year and telling me about everything she was learning. It fascinated me. As I mentioned earlier, for seven years now, men and women from around the country have joined us in going through this Bible together in a closed Facebook group.

In her book, *Out of Sorts,* author Sarah Bessey tells her readers, "I speak in tongues and I pray the hours. I dance and clap at church, but I also sit in silence and meditation. I place my hands on people when I pray for them, and I light candles. I follow the church calendar observing Lent and Pentecost, Advent and ordinary time, but I worship in community with believers who do not—and likely never will—and I belong there."

That's what I've discovered too. The people in my church family have a faith that isn't just like mine. Thank goodness. Believe me, you don't have to go down the road to the Moravian church to find someone who believes differently than you do—take a look at the person in the pew beside you. I'm blessed in that I do have a wonderful group of women who are willing to explore other spiritual practices with me. That's a big part of the women's ministry picture I see in front of me today—tell us more about all the ways we can worship Jesus together. Who knows, maybe we can talk some of the men into journeying with us too.

When I first started writing about faith, I didn't know exactly where it would take me. One of the things I've discovered I love to write about, and read about, are people's faith journeys, particularly as they practice various spiritual disciplines and attend a variety of churches. Church stories. A friend of mine has attended the same church since birth. That's more than fifty years now in one church. What is missing from a church experience that has people go church shopping, or leaving church altogether?

People offer all kinds of answers. People want community-focused churches. There's not enough discipleship. We demand better music. We seek deeper liturgy. They long for a tradition that reminds them of our ancient ties. They want a contemporary service so they don't get bored. Weekends are filled with sports and other activities. Sundays are the only days a family can stay home. Could this be summed up by saying we're wired to long for a deep connection to a church that draws us closer to God? When we don't find that, off we go. Except, we've all heard it before, when you feel distant from God, he's not the one who moved.

Blogging has been an incredible journey. Through reading other blogs, I have discovered some amazing writers, and many of them are writing about the same things I'm passionate about . . . church and faith. They introduced me to a whole world of Christianity I didn't know a thing about . . . liturgy and the church calendar. I read about people who don't take communion the same way I do. One author told about the time she spent at a monastery. A former Southern Baptist wrote about his days at Baylor University (a Southern Baptist school), and his break from the faith traditions of his childhood into the priesthood as an Episcopalian. One of my favorite writers, who I discovered three years ago, grew up charismatic, but found a deeper, renewed faith as she read ancient theologians who taught her about the church calendar. Two other authors struggled mightily with the evangelical movement we grew up in, rebelling against it to the point they didn't know if they could continue to call this large group of Christians their brothers and sisters in Christ. This larger group of evangelical Christians who loved me so well had gravely disappointed them.

As I read about these faith experiences, I began to realize what my own faith was missing. Not a perfect church or a return to my

Southern Baptist roots or a plunge into a radically new faith practice. What I wanted was more of Jesus, however I could find him. That idea caused me to evaluate my faith up to this point. Where had I found Jesus before now? In a Methodist church on an old gravel road in Missouri; on the faces of friends-also-family at Mt. Pleasant; when my family brought our collective broken hearts to First Baptist, because we were tired of seeing pastors being let go; at my Catholic friend's house in high school; in that little community a few miles away from my childhood home, where the Mennonites live set apart for God; at the megachurch Second Baptist, led by one of the godliest men I've ever had the privilege of knowing; among the charismatics, who saved my brother from a lifestyle of sin; over a glass of beer, discussing theology with my single friends in St. Louis; in a fresh, surprising way on the face of Pastor Bob, who preached because life had given him a theology degree; just last Sunday, when Larry led us in worship, and Pastor Jason got up afterward and spoke straight from scripture and from his heart.

I'd seen Jesus in so many places, and so many traditions, and realizing this broke something free in me. I determined to learn how other Christians worshiped Jesus. I attended an Ash Wednesday service with the Catholics and a stations of the cross service with the Episcopalians and wrote about them. There's a small Methodist church in the town where we live now, and I sometimes attend there when I am free of obligations at my own church. The first time I stepped into their sanctuary, memories of the country churches in my childhood overwhelmed me. They have a main sanctuary full of pews, but then a side section with pews as well. The services there remind me of the ones I attended at Mt. Olive. They serve up communion with bread freshly baked by women in the church, not entirely different from the way Colleen and her mom baked the bread on a pizza pan, as she told us about in chapter 1. Maybe we'll have communion with warm, homemade bread in heaven. For the first time, I attended church on the Day of Pentecost, with these United Methodists. Well, obviously I had attended church on Pentecost Sunday for years prior, but this was the first time I heard it acknowledged. I was there one Sunday when they baptized an infant, and I loved the way a congregation and family came together, promising to raise this child to know God.

One fall, while on vacation, I dragged my cousin with me to a small church in northern Michigan. I don't remember their particular faith tradition, but I'm pretty sure they had never heard of Willow Creek or its vast database of churches. It was a friendly church, and they were served by a husband/wife pastoral team. She preached that day. Another vacation, a friend and I visited a Lutheran church. For the first time, I had wine for communion. This particular friend grew up Catholic, and she recognized more of the liturgical parts of the service than I did. We had a lovely visit with the priest and her husband at the church luncheon after the service. She explained to us how in a community their size, it doesn't make sense for the churches to offer individual ministries to their congregants. So they've partnered up with the five area churches in town to minister together. The pastoral leaders even share pulpits with one another. I remembered the ecumenical community services I had attended at my home church, First Baptist, during Holy Week, my sophomore year of college. I knew God was pleased to see these churches working together.

At home, we've observed Advent and Lent. When our daughter was a toddler, I wrote a daily reading for each part of the Christmas story. Using an Advent tree, we read each morning before she opened the door for candy, a coin, or some trinket. I have watched her blossom into a reader each year as we've used these simple readings. She looks the scripture passages up on her own now. I've offered to find a more age-appropriate book for her but no, the toddler readings have become a tradition. As a family, we light candles of an Advent wreath on those blustery Sunday nights of December.

For Lent, our family talks about what we're going to give up (last year it was limited time on social media for me) and what we're going to add. The final week, Holy Week, we read through what Jesus did each day. My daughter and I have attended stations of the cross services a number of times. Last year, my church had an evening service each day and on Holy Saturday, I attended my first Easter vigil at the local Catholic church. On my blog, tracesoffaith.com, I did a series exploring forty hymn stories, some history and some personal narratives from myself and friends. What a meaningful way for my readers to prepare their hearts for Easter Sunday.

I've asked my husband to build me a prayer bench (the French call it a *prie-dieu*). I wrote a review for a book about a man who makes pilgrimages to Mt. Athos, a mountain holy to the Orthodox in Greece. To show his appreciation for the kind review, he sent me a prayer rope blessed by a monk. I use it often in my private prayer time. Orthodox Christianity isn't what I'm used to. Yet as I read about this ancient tradition dating back to the days of Jesus's apostles, I find pieces I'm familiar with in my own life, the celebration of events like nativity, Jesus's baptism and resurrection, the singing of hymns, fasting and feasting, Holy Communion (or Eucharist). Always communion. I recognize church.

Meet Phoebe

I'm excited to tell you about Phoebe, because she's the first friend I made who is a Christian practicing in the Coptic Orthodox tradition. She gifted me a small white booklet entitled *Agpia: The Prayer Book of the Canonical Hours*. In the accompanying notecard, after the thoughtful, personal note, she signed it, "Your sister in Christ." In the midst of this journey I'm on, those four words meant everything. Here, Phoebe writes about the observance of the Christian season, Epiphany, which for Coptic Orthodox Christians commemorates the baptism of Christ and the divine revelation of the Holy Trinity. For Western Christians observing the church calendar, Epiphany marks the arrival of the wise men in Bethlehem as metaphor for Jesus being known by the whole world, and is celebrated on January 6th or the Sunday following. It's like nothing I've ever celebrated, but Phoebe does a good job of explaining it, and she's always gracious to answer any questions I have about what I'm learning:

> Epiphany, the great feast of the manifestation of the divinity of Our Lord Jesus Christ, is now often overshadowed by

the Nativity, but was celebrated by Christians long before we started celebrating the Nativity. While all of the major feasts of our Lord are preceded by long fasts and celebrated with sumptuous meals, the Epiphany in the Coptic Orthodox church is preceded only by one day of fasting, and is then celebrated with a traditional dish known as *ol'ass*, oranges (and making orange lanterns), and in Egypt, sugar cane.

Let me start by describing what Epiphany is like in church. The service begins at night—like Nativity and the Resurrection—but starts with a "Liturgy of the Waters," during which water in a large basin (*laqqan*), symbolizing the Jordan River, is blessed, all the congregation is blessed with the water, and then small bottles are handed out to the congregation to take home. In Egypt, at least until the tenth century before this public practice was banned, the entire community, Muslim and Christian, would celebrate this part of the liturgy together, and process together to the Nile to bless the waters and throw in a wooden cross. Many even jumped into the Nile, believing it could heal their sicknesses. Children would make orange lanterns by coring an orange, carving out a cross on both sides, and placing a small candle in them to light the way to the Nile. The candles symbolized the light they received in their baptism, and the oil that is released when pressure is put on the orange peel symbolizes the oil of the Holy Chrismation, which they received by anointing after baptism. Although this large community procession no longer happens, many households, including mine, will create orange lanterns to mark the feast.

After the Liturgy of the Waters, the Divine Liturgy begins. Hymns on Epiphany are sung in the joyous tone, and congregational responses include this special Epiphany response, "Jesus Christ the Son of God was baptized in the Jordan." The Epiphany prayer right before communion reminds us of our own baptism: "You have bestowed upon us the grace of sonship, through the washing of rebirth and the newness of the

Holy Spirit." At around midnight we take communion, then head home for a traditional Epiphany feast.

Taro root and oranges are in season in Egypt during Epiphany, but there is another reason why *ol'ass*—a green stew of beef, taro root (*coloccasia*), and swiss chard—is eaten on this day. Taro root is toxic if eaten raw because it contains calcium oxaltate, which can make the mouth and throat go numb and is linked to kidney stones. It must therefore be fully cooked by boiling it in water to be edible—and once cooked, it's a superfood, full of fiber and other important nutrients. Quite like what happens to us when we are baptized—we throw off the corruption of sin and become transformed into sons of God through Christ Jesus (Galatians 3:27). We also taste good—like salt to the earth (Matthew 5:13).

It is difficult to get sugar cane in the United States, at least here in the Northeast, and I'm not sure why sugar cane is also eaten on Epiphany in Egypt, other than it being in season. To eat sugar cane you must peel off the hard outer shell and suck out the sweet liquid with your teeth. It can also be pressed through iron rolls to create sugar cane juice, a very popular drink in Egypt—there are shops devoted just to selling sugar cane juice. I often meditate and assume that perhaps the sweet taste of the liquid inside the hard outer shell reminds us of the sweetness of Christ himself, taking a human form on our behalf and suffering as we suffer, so that we may have eternal life, and so that we may "taste and see that the Lord is good" (Psalm 34:8). Or, perhaps it served to remind Christians, especially those in Egypt who faced and continue to face persecution, that just as pressing sugar cane through iron rolls leads to sweet sugar cane juice, so "we are hard-pressed on every side, yet not crushed; we are perplexed, but not in despair; persecuted, but not forsaken; struck down, but not destroyed—always carrying about in the body the dying of the Lord Jesus, that the life of Jesus also may be manifested in our body" (2 Corinthians 4:8-10).

The Orthodox observance of Epiphany is a lot to digest! There's so much more I want to explore. What on earth (or heavens) are the Orthodox doing? I have no idea but when I emailed a local Antiochian priest, he said I could visit anytime. In fact, he told me several professors and others affiliated with the local Christian colleges also ask him if they can visit.

In Frederica Mathews-Green's book, *Facing East: A Pilgrim's Journey into the Mysteries of Orthodoxy,* the author shares a story about a Forgiveness Vespers she attended. In an evening service that begins Great Lent, congregants form two lines, facing each other. One by one starting with the priest, each person looks in the eyes of the person across from them and asks forgiveness for any wrongdoing they may have done to the other individual.

"One at a time I bow to people I worship with every week, looking each one in the eye, men and women, children and aged. Each interchange is an intimate moment, and I feel on the wobbly border between embarrassment, laughter, and tears. Just to pause and look at each fellow worshiper for a moment, to see the individual there, is itself a startling exercise."

I went to a Forgiveness Vespers. I met a woman in a Facebook community group who attended that Antiochian church near me. She offered to let me sit with her. The pastor said to visit any time I wanted. They invited me. I took them up on it.

When the time came to line up and say the words "forgive me" or "forgive me, a sinner," I participated. It's what I do. I join up with Christians in a variety of traditions, believing Christ is among us. I didn't know a single person as I went down the line, asking forgiveness. Still, in a big picture way, don't we all need to ask forgiveness of one another? One by one, they assured me "God forgives." Afterward, my friend sent me a private message on Facebook. Apparently, they talked about the "new girl" after I left. She wrote, "Everyone thought you were extremely brave."

I don't know about brave. What I do know is Orthodox Christians experience Jesus in unique ways. I'm missing out on encounters with my Savior because I am unfamiliar with their practices. I want to know about every way I can experience Jesus. Quite simply, I'll take Jesus anywhere I can find him.

Church, what if we really saw one another as individuals looking for more of Jesus? I grew up thinking Catholics worshiped God (and Mary) all wrong. In recent years, I've read about and discussed, with actual Catholics, the meaning behind their spiritual practices. A devout Catholic who understands the traditions she's observing has a beautiful faith.

So, taking notes from Eastern Orthodox Christians, I would stand before a Catholic and say, "Forgive me for not taking the time to learn about how you worship. Out of ignorance, for much of my life, I made a lot of false judgments."

Who would you stand before and ask forgiveness?

Once I decided to approach fellow Christ-followers with listening ears and an open heart, I kept seeing more and more opportunities to experience Christ in new ways.

The next time I'm invited to a charismatic revival meeting, I'm going. I want to attend an Amish church service. One of these years, I'm going to talk my daughter into foregoing the big bang on Christmas morning, and opening one gift a day for the twelve days of Christmas. I want to do a weekend retreat of silence at a monastery. I desperately want to go on a pilgrimage somewhere, maybe the Camino de Santiago. I have a Nigerian friend who grew up observing Levitical law in his church community and I want to know more, lots more, about that. My friend went to a community-wide, ecumenical Ash Wednesday service at a park in Kalamazoo a few years back, and I want to join her there sometime. God has planted a dream in my heart to conduct a monthly service, using formal liturgy, and incorporating times of silent prayer, lament, and *lectio divina* readings, in my own church. My mom brought me a prayer shawl from Israel, and I imagine the holiness of reciting a prayer in Hebrew, with the linen cloth sheltering my head and my heart from the rest of the world. I love the idea of having a mezuzah in the doorframe of my home, touching it often as I come and go, reciting these words from the Shema, "Hear, O Israel: the Lord our God, the Lord is one. . . ." At a conference in 2014, I heard an author speak about her experience growing up on a vineyard in Germany. She's convinced we're looking at the gift of wine God gave us the wrong way, and she wrote a book about it. I'm inclined to agree with her. Another author wrote an incredible book about his journeys to three separate religious organizations who have ministries where they grow food, in an effort to reacquaint themselves with the earth God asked us to care for—I do a little gardening myself, so I'd be delighted to visit with groups like this and implement some of their practices with my local congregation.

The Southern Baptists didn't teach me about any of this. I'm thinking it surely must be because they don't know either. We can all live within our own church walls. Individual faith traditions are powerful infrastructures. I have friends who couldn't do anything fun, like riding a bike or swimming at the lake, as kids on a Sunday because it was the Sabbath. My heart goes out to men and women who have been abused by the hands of clergy (Lord, have mercy). It's also true I talk with people who have been disillusioned at the very least, if not outright injured, by the legalism and/or mundaneness of church practices—women who can recite every responsive portion of a Catholic Mass, but couldn't tell you what a word of it means, men who know every line of the Apostles Creed, yet couldn't articulate what their own everyday faith looks like. What I have found, though, and what many friends on my journey have discovered as well, is that these religious practices do have meaning. The words are incredibly beautiful and capable of bringing us into the presence of God. Icons exist not to worship an image, but as a visual means to join us to the holiness of God and his saints. Like many of the spiritual objects and practices I've learned about, they help to right our focus. The world is distracting. The Sabbath is the first thing God called holy, and he did so over and over and over again. I do think he wants us to set it apart as holy, without assigning suffocating do's and don'ts to it. Even if the practices of a certain tradition have hurt you deeply, can you ask God to show you where Jesus was in your faith at that time? May he bring to mind what was beautiful about the beginning, and maybe you can build on that. Surely God wants us to be a church who gets along with one another, teaching each other new and exciting ways to worship Jesus.

A friend of mine who attended First Baptist with me as a child joined a Presbyterian church when she lived in Oklahoma. Like me, she was introduced to the church calendar. She participated in things like Advent, Lent, and ordinary time, from the Latin term *tempus per annum* (literally "time through the year"), which takes up more than half of the liturgical year. She got married and moved back home. Her precious little family of four chose to return to First Baptist, but she still privately practices the various parts of the church calendar on her own occasionally. I've often wondered if I would have made the same choice she did, if I returned to our hometown. Could I be a Southern Baptist again, having acquired so much knowledge about other spiritual disciplines and theological differences? I'm not the only person who has left behind the faith tradition of their childhood to have asked these questions. I treasure these words from Scott Cairns, author of *Short Trip to the Edge*, who converted from Baptist to Greek Orthodox in his adult years. "Even now, on occasion, I wonder if the best choice wouldn't have been to stay put. It certainly would have been the more aggravating choice, but I wonder if the braver choice would have been to remain in that besieged community where I was first taught the love of God, where I might have taken part in that community's recovery of a fullness that's been more or less left behind—as it were—by historical aberration and unfortunate, reactionary choice."

As for me, my answer is yes. I would join the Southern Baptists of my younger days, if they'd have me. They loved me so well and instilled a love for scripture in me. Those women who prepared food for the potlucks of my childhood served up the best meatloaf I've ever tasted. At times, I really miss those potlucks. I long for worship services that end with an altar call. For forty-some years, these people have remained a part of my life, even from hundreds of miles away. And by the grace of God, I've found a church family in Michigan as well. Do we always agree? Of course not. Regardless, it is this church where I have committed to be ministered to and to serve.

Furthermore, I think we have to learn what we can agree to disagree on and still be Christians. I was pleased to come across an Anglican document, the Chicago-Lambeth Quadrilateral, suggesting the same concept back in 1886 (you can find this document in the 1979 Book of Common Prayer). A priest by the name of William Reed Huntington came up with four points Christian traditions must agree on:

1. The Holy Scriptures, as containing all things necessary to salvation;
2. The creeds (specifically, the Apostles' and Nicene Creeds) as the sufficient statement of Christian faith;
3. The dominical sacraments of baptism and Holy Communion;
4. The historical episcopate, locally adapted.

In an admirable ecumenical effort, this resolution agreed to the following four things:

1. Our earnest desire that the Savior's prayer, "That we may all be one," may, in its deepest and truest sense, be speedily fulfilled;
2. That we believe that all who have been duly baptized with water, in the name of the Father, and of the Son, and of the Holy Ghost, are members of the holy catholic church;
3. That in all things of human ordering or human choice, relating to modes of worship and discipline, or to traditional customs, this church is ready in the spirit of love and humility to forego all preferences of her own;
4. That this church does not seek to absorb other communions, but rather, co-operating with them on the basis of a common faith and order, to discountenance schism, to heal the wounds of the body of Christ, and to promote the charity which is the chief of Christian graces and the visible manifestation of Christ to the world.

A friend of mine used to say, "I'm a baptist with a little b, a Christian with a capital C." That's it. North Point is my church family. What they offer me in the way of spiritual practices and liturgical worship isn't enough. One church can't offer me enough. Not this side of glory. I think when we allow for more mystery in our faith, it has room to breathe. Breath is life. Breath is spirit. None of us have God figured out, though God doesn't seem to mind this one bit. But together, we can seek more. It's why I explore, and what I've discovered awakens a thirst in me for more and more living water. Also holy water and fresh loaves of homemade communion bread.

That Jesus the churches of my childhood introduced me to all those years ago? He is mighty big and he is everywhere. He's been in every Christian tradition I've experienced. Not in every person who attends church. Not in every church in every tradition. Rely on the Holy Spirit to guide you in your efforts. Ask for discernment as you seek new ways to ignite your own faith. Study the creeds for yourself; throw in various catechisms for additional knowledge. Study the Bible and pray with other Christ-followers. Go expecting to meet brothers and sisters in Christ. Please bring some of what you learn back home to your own church. Most importantly, go fully confident you're about to receive more of Jesus.

Epilogue

Better Together

In the beginning, as in the earliest days of the church, Christians were simply followers of the way, or Nazarenes. Luke tells us this in Acts. After Christianity's separation from Judaism in the first century, there was no initial separation of Protestant, Orthodox, and Catholic. No Russian this or Greek that, although our location on the globe would naturally influence how we worshiped. No Methodist, Baptist, Lutheran, Pentecostal, Reformed, Presbyterian, Mennonite, Village, or (fill in the blank). Can you imagine worshiping on a church pew in a basilica, with a Pentecostal speaking in tongues on your right and an Orthodox believer venerating an icon as they enter from the narthex? What if the only name you knew these fellow believers by was . . . Christian? The Nicene and Apostles' creeds were written well before the church split into Catholic and Orthodox believers. These words that thousands of churches around the world still recite in our worship services will always call out to us—come together under these core beliefs. For one thousand years, the church in all its vast difference, amidst persecution, numerous councils to determine what a Christ-follower should believe, and in the process of identifying heretical teachings, we were one catholic (universal) church.

The more I interact with the church, my heart longs for a unity, even when we don't agree. A healing. What Christ himself prayed for us:

> [I pray] that they may all be one. As you, Father, are in me and I am in you, may they also be in us, so that the world may believe that you have sent me.
>
> John 17:21

I have developed a passion for visiting church traditions other than my own. Why do Roman Catholics, Anglicans, and others walk around one day a year with ashes in the shape of a cross marked on their forehead? Do Lutherans, Catholics, Episcopalians, and many others really offer actual wine at the communion table? These are all stories I've shared with you in this book.

I don't know if we'll ever get there, but I long for a day when we can worship with all our Christian brothers and sisters at the same table. From everything I've read, to the conversations I've had, and the various services I've attended, Christ has gotten so much bigger to me. So. Much. Bigger. Dear readers, we are missing out if we don't expand our belief system to learn from Christians who worship in other ways. Is Jesus big enough to help us look beyond our differences? I think so. Lord, help my unbelief.

Contributors

Leslie Albizzatti is in several writing groups with me on Facebook. She blogs at seekanduwillfind.com.

Quantrilla Ard is a writer but also a wife, homeschooling mama, and a doctoral student. She blogs at thephdmamma.com.

Crystal Brandenberger is a friend of a friend. We have not met in person but she graciously agreed to share her experience within the Amish community.

Ed Cyzewski is a writer whose books include *Flee, Be Silent, Pray: Ancient Prayers for Anxious Christians,* and *A Christian Survival Guide: A Lifeline to Faith and Growth.* Ed blogs at edcyzewski.com.

Reba Land is a wife, mom, and kindergarten teacher. I appreciate her unique perspective on Christianity as a lifelong charismatic.

Pauline Magnusson is an online friend. She's always willing to share her experience as a Roman Catholic who converted to Eastern Orthodoxy. I'm thrilled to include her essay here.

Phoebe Mikhail is the author of *Putting Joy into Practice: Seven Ways to Lift Your Spirit from the Early Church.* She blogs at beingin community.com.

Amy Repp is a family friend. Our families meet up for a visit a couple times every year. She always brings cookies from the Cookie Cottage in Fort Wayne.

Rhonda Robertson is a childhood neighbor and friend. She too spent time playing at Mt. Olive Church, the church who never locked its doors.

Ronne Rock is the author of *One Woman Can Change the World: Reclaiming Your God-Designed Influence and Impact Right Where You Are*. She blogs at ronnerock.com.

Sarah (not her real name) shares an essay in chapter 3. She has requested her identity remain anonymous.

Aaron Smith is the author of *Cultural Savage: The Intersection of Christianity and Mental Illness*. He blogs at culturalsavage.com.

Bailey Suzio also lives in Michigan and sometimes we meet for coffee in real life. She blogs regularly at thethinplace.net.

Colleen Stout is a local friend. You can read about her humorous yet insightful travels around Michigan at thismichiganlife.com.

Nicole Walters is a writer whose essay appeared in the anthology *Everbloom: Stories of Deeply Rooted and Transformed Lives*. She blogs at nicoletwalters.com.

Donnie Williams was sent my way by a friend on Facebook. He is Bureau Chief for the Office of Inspector General, North Bureau of Investigations.

References

These are books I mentioned (in order of appearance)—you may appreciate them as well.

Shauna Niequist, *Bread and Wine: A Love Letter to Life around the Table with Recipes* (Grand Rapids, MI: Zondervan, 2017), 17.

Lauren Winner, *Girl Meets God* (New York: Random House, 2002), 85.

Austin Channing Brown, *I'm Still Here: Black Dignity in a World Made for Whiteness* (New York: Convergent Books, 2018), 39.

Micha Boyett, *Found: A Story of Questions, Grace, and Everyday Prayer* (Franklin, TN: Worthy Publishing, 2014), 50.

Sarah Bessey, *Out of Sorts: Making Peace with an Evolving Faith* (New York: Howard Books, 2015), 151.

Frederica Mathewes-Greene, *Facing East: A Pilgrim's Journey into the Mysteries of Orthodoxy* (San Francisco: HarperOne, 2006), 20.

Scott Cairns, *Short Trip to the Edge: A Pilgrimage to Prayer* (Brewster, MA: Paraclete Press, 2016), 226.

Acknowledgments

We don't go to church alone, do we? Books aren't an individual project either. Don't get me wrong, there are whole days and weeks when the work is lonely and done in the quiet, but this book has been lived out my whole life.

To the people of Mt. Pleasant Church, thank you for teaching me that Jesus loves me. I've never forgotten this truth and it carries me.

To Mt. Olive, that beloved church up the road from my childhood home, I'm forever grateful for your open doors.

To First Baptist, who welcomed my family when we were without a church home, I first started spreading my faith wings inside your church walls.

A friend on Twitter once joked, "How do you solve a problem like Traci?" as a nod to the lovely but confused Maria von Trapp of *Sound of Music* fame. North Point, you let me explore and share what I find with you. I'm sure there are times you're not sure what to do with me, but I'm glad to be part of a church that seeks him.

So many others. To our pastors, I hope you feel seen in the pages of this book. We need your faithfulness and guidance and integrity. To my mom and brothers, you're right there in some of the best church memories I have. To my Wednesday night Bible study women, you are a highlight of every week. To the children I teach in Sunday school and vacation Bible school, stay in church and in God's word. He is worthy. To those who contributed essays for this book, it's a better project with your stories in it. To the readers at tracesoffaith.com, thanks for reading along the way as this book took form blog post by blog post. To my agent Jim Hart, thank you for taking on an unknown author and not giving up on me. To the team at Church Publishing, under Nancy Bryan's expert guidance, what an absolute pleasure to publish my first book with you. To my writing friends, I've found a group who gets me. Let's keep sharing in our successes big and small! To Ms. Margnet, the first person to see the words in this book, because I needed a reader who would love it and boost my confidence.

To my daughter, the cry of my heart is to pass on to you a church that shines ever more brightly with the glory of Christ. To my husband, I still remember one of the first gifts you ever gave me, a subscription to *Writer's Digest.* You've always supported my dream, and no one's "congratulations" means more to me than yours.

About the Author

Writer and Bible teacher Traci Rhoades has called nine different churches over four denominations and six locales her home church. This varied experience has given her a unique perspective on church life, fueling a passion for exploring all the ways Christians worship Jesus. A Missouri native, she now lives with her husband and daughter in rural Michigan. She enjoys frequenting local eateries, reading just about anything, talking church, and winning card games. Visit her online at www.tracesoffaith.com and on Twitter @tracesoffaith.

Illustrator: A. Rhoades